BRIEF COACHING FOR LASTING SOLUTIONS

More Advance Acclaim for
Brief Coaching for Lasting Solutions

"Elegant solution construction is the essence of all great coaching. At last! Here is a book on coaching from the founders of the brief solution-focused approach. Insoo Kim Berg and Peter Szabó provide an outstanding methodology for applying solution-focused principles to a wide range of coaching situations. Easy to read, jargon-free, and packed with real-life case studies, this book will be of great value to all coaches who want to extend their understanding of solution-focused coaching, and to anyone who wants to understand and use solution-focused principles in their work or their personal lives. Enjoy!"
—Anthony M. Grant, Ph..D., Director, Coaching Psychology Unit, University of Sydney

"Insoo Kim Berg and Peter Szabó have created a wonderful book rich with deceptively simple techniques and strategies for developing the art of quality coaching. Building on theories from Solution Focused Therapy, they have applied many of the future-oriented strategies and interventions in nonclinical contexts. Although many coaches and clients obviously will find great value in a longer term relationship, brief coaching principles apply to all great coaching, whether it involves one session or many sessions. This book is a great addition to the library of coaches and consultants."
—Patrick Williams, Ed.D., Master Certified Coach and coauthor of *Therapist as Life Coach, Total Life Coaching,* and *Law and Ethics in Coaching*

A Norton Professional Book

BRIEF COACHING FOR LASTING SOLUTIONS

INSOO KIM BERG AND PETER SZABÓ

W·W·NORTON

NEW YORK · LONDON

For information about permission to reproduce
selections from this book, write to
Permissions, W. W. Norton & Company, Inc.
500 Fifth Avenue, New York, NY 10110

Composition and book design by Viewtistic, Inc.
Manufacturing by Fairfield Graphics
Production Manager: Leeann Graham

Library of Congress Cataloging-in-Publication Data

Berg, Insoo Kim.
  Brief coaching for lasting solutions / Insoo Kim Berg and Peter Szabó.
    p. cm.
  "A Norton professional book."
  Includes bibliographical references and index.
  ISBN 0-393-70472-6
  1. Executive coaching. 2. Personal coaching. 3. Counseling. I. Szabó,
Peter. II. Title.

HD30.4.B48 2005
658.4'07124—dc22   2005048245

W. W. Norton & Company, Inc., 500 Fifth Avenue, New York, NY 10110
www.wwnorton.com

W.W. Norton & Company, Inc., 15 Carlisle Street, London
W1D 3BS

10 9 8

To Stephanie, my loving coach through life, and my children Anna-Julia, Tabea, and Till who are looking forward to reading their names here.

Peter Szabó

To Steve, my friend, partner, coach, and mentor. Thank you.

To Sarah, thank you for your life-long coaching in my effort to be a parent.

Insoo Kim Berg

CONTENTS

PREFACE

Coaching could be defined as, "Comfortably bringing important people from where they are to where they want to be." This definition dates back to the times when a coach was a means of transportation pulled by a team of horses, and traveling was a long and arduous undertaking. Even though our desire to travel in comfort has remained the same, we also want to reach our destination quickly and effectively. This desire to go from point A to point B with comfort and speed is what a modern-day coach works with. Often clients want to reach and exceed their goals, visions, and dreams in their personal or work life.

Many books about coaching are on the market—books about how to build a successful coaching practice, books with checklists to follow through with clients, books on sports coaching, executive coaching, personal coaching, and many other specific applications. You may have been searching for a guidebook that will teach you how to practice coaching in a way that is easy to understand, with many useful skills you can adapt to use in variety of settings. Of course, you would want the guidebook to be simple and the learning process easy to master, sensible, and, most of all, effective in producing the desired outcome. That is, you just want it to work, and it is reasonable to ask for a book to do so. Having talked to hundreds of practitioners over the years, we have learned that most people in the helping professions have been drawn to this field by the desire to make a difference in someone's life. By doing so, perhaps we may even change the world.

This book is written for coaching practitioners who want to make a difference in the world, however small, who want to be effective while being respectful of what the client brings to the table, and who want to work with important resources that clients already have. This book is particularly useful for coaching professionals who are interested in reducing the time necessary for bringing clients to where they want to be.

We hope that this book is exactly what you have been looking for, whether you want to sharpen and hone the skills you have acquired over the years, or whether you are in the midst of a transition in your profession or career and want to start from the beginning. To keep things comfortable for you while you are traveling in this coaching territory, we have created sidebars and boxes with reminders, tips from the field of coaching, answers to questions from the field, and ways to feed your passion for doing the right thing for clients.

Fresh perspectives always make it possible to stretch our minds and enhance our skills. Traveling to unfamiliar land or returning to familiar and stimulating sites does the same. We hope this book will rekindle your passion for retooling your skills and getting on with the job of empowering clients. We will address you as an expert who has all the abilities, resources, and solutions necessary for reaching your own goals as a coach. We will reinforce you in making the most out of what you already have in your backpack for your journey. But we promise you that the journey will not always be smooth. It will challenge your mind and stretch your imagination. Most of all, you may end up scratching your head from time to time, puzzled about how such simple things might work so well.

Of course, we also intend to frequently tap on your shoulder and direct your attention to new directions and different perspectives. You are invited to play with a greater variety of choices in your coaching tools so that you can more easily discover ways to make your work brief and effective. We will accompany you step by step as you become well acquainted with the brief coaching approach and help you gain confidence to apply what you will learn.

One warning, however, is that while the concept is simple and seems like common sense that everybody already has, it is not easy to master the techniques—not because they are complicated and complex to learn, but because they require a highly disciplined mind-set to remain simple when problems seem too complicated and difficult. Many people mistakenly and think that being complex and complicated will serve the client better, often resulting in long-term coaching and feeling lost from time to time. Again, staying simple takes a great deal of discipline and skills.

The central topic of the book is the coaching conversation: how to conduct conversations that are most useful for the client in getting results within a brief period of time. Many master coaches have one thing in common: A certain conviction about the clients they work with and a strong belief in clients' ability to figure out what is good for themselves and what they want to achieve.

In Chapter 1, we introduce how brief coaching is conceptualized and why even the most complex problem can be solved in a brief period of contact. It is all related to looking at things from "outside the box." Once you step out of the box, then you need to be clear about what you believe about the clients you work with, because learning techniques does not guarantee successful coaching unless your heart is in the right place. Using a single case, we describe detailed conversational strategies to set the tone for a brief coaching session. The section "Getting Started" explains all the little strategies as well as tools.

We devote Chapter 2 to language strategies and useful tools that you can use to set the tone for the first session. Setting realistic, measurable goals and negotiating the road map that will help the client get started in the right direction are described with various case examples. This chapter is primarily about what to do and ways to empower clients to come up with their own solutions that will fit their own culture, values, and worldview according to what makes sense to them. Surprisingly, we also address ways to negotiate the outcome of the session before you begin the coaching activities.

In Chapter 3, we discuss the second half of the first meeting, when you will wrap up the session and summarize what you heard during the session. Suggestions for many creative experiments that will help clients reach their goals are laid out. What to do in second, third, and later sessions, as well as what to do when there is no progress, is described in detail.

All coaches face infrequent but still difficult situations that creep into our practices and consume enormous amounts of time and energy. Chapter 4 is devoted to managing mandated clients who are sent to us against their wishes, clients in intense conflict, and some who want us to change other people who make their lives difficult, as well as clients who feel caught between two or more equally attractive choices.

Chapter 5 addresses topics and issues that surface less frequently in coaching but are just as important, such as crises, emergencies, and setbacks.

To help further your skill building, along with this book, we have collaborated to create a DVD demonstration of a live interview with a client. It is available through Brief Family Therapy Center in Milwaukee, Wisconsin.

Cases in the book are composites of real cases (with names and circumstances changed to guarantee client confidentiality). Some small dialogues are recreated for the book.

BRIEF COACHING FOR LASTING SOLUTIONS

CHAPTER ONE

GETTING STARTED

As the name implies, brief coaching is about being brief. Coaching occurs through a specialized conversation the coach has with clients with the intention to support them and give them a good start in their journey to find what they are seeking. Brief coaching, in addition, is possible through a focused conversation designed to help clients stay focused on their goals. The conversation does not end either in a designated time frame or after a number of sessions agreed upon, but when clients feel confident that they can travel the rest of the journey on their own without the coach's guidance or companionship.

> **HOT QUOTATION**
> "Problem talk creates problems—solution talk creates solutions."
> —*Steve De Shazer*

Another important characteristic is that brief coaching utilizes what clients bring to the coaching relationship and conversation; that is, they already have skills, views, and many other tools. This is vastly different from looking at client deficits and trying to augment or add on what they are lacking. Because we view clients as competent, resourceful, resilient, experts on their life and work situations, the task of coaching is to build on these existing resources. Therefore, when you follow some of the steps we outline here, the coaching can be brief, but the outcome will be long-lasting.

Whether your clients want to achieve a single specific goal or a broad vision, make progress in work and personal life balance issues, become more effective in empowering employees, find themselves in better career positions, or simply develop hidden potentials, most clients are eager to get going on their road to success. Perhaps your clients are suddenly confronted with a situation that got out of control, such as a threatening conflict or a temporary workload that they do not know how to deal with. They will be grateful to find support and reorient themselves in getting back in touch with their resources and competencies with speed and efficiency. Thus, the brief coaching skills described in this book can be very useful in many situations that call for an efficient and effective approach to making changes.

Even if you work with longer-term contracts with regularly scheduled coaching sessions, or if you offer assessments and follow up with personal development plans, brief coaching skills can be useful to get a head start with your client and experience the satisfaction of observing positive changes that are sustained over a longer period of time.

INTRODUCING ELIZABETH

Twenty-seven-year-old Elizabeth walked into our office hesitantly, as if she was not sure that she wanted to do this and perhaps found it difficult. But she looked determined to follow through, now that she had walked in the door. She sat down and explained that she could not bear the stress of the workplace and her coworkers anymore, even though she loved the job she was doing. She needed help quickly because she had suffered from coworker harassment for too long already. It was affecting her job performance because she could not concentrate, could not sleep well at night, and dreaded facing her coworkers every morning. Trying to pretend that it did not affect her had not helped at all—if anything, it made things worse for her.

During the painful description of her daily stresses, we discovered that in spite of the dread and what seemed like the monumental task walking into the office every morning, once she got to her desk and was faced with a big pile of work, she could forget about her coworkers and concentrate on her work. Although she was worried that her boss would soon notice that her productivity was dropping, he had not given her any direct indication that this was the case so far. If anything, Elizabeth indicated that he had increased her responsibility on the job, which of course she liked very much. The job market was tight in her field because many companies were downsizing and merging, and she could almost talk herself into a panic. She could imagine herself without a job, losing her apartment, and all the other disastrous events that would unfold. We agreed that these were her fears and she had not heard any direct warning or anything to indicate that she might be on the verge of losing her job.

She related that she had tried to figure out what was causing her coworkers to be so difficult to get along with. They treated her as if she had some kind of contagious disease. They would become quiet when she approached them or just passed by; they had lunch with each other in the cafeteria every day but never invited her to sit with them. They never asked her about her personal life or her new boyfriend, nor were they interested in small talk with her, nor did they tell her about their weekends or what they did on vacation.

Recognizing that she was well-educated and quite intelligent, she had tried to figure out what might be the problem. "Is it my personality? Is it something about me?" she asked herself a hundred times. Did she do something to offend one of them without meaning to? Was it her cultural heritage they detested? Was it because they thought her boss gave her more slack with deadlines or sick days? Were they conspiring against her because they were jealous about her boyfriend, who sent flowers to her office on special occasions? She decided that was far-fetched, since they had not even met Bill, her boyfriend. Maybe it was because she had moved up faster than they had and she might be on the way to get more promotions. Could it be because she had more credentials than they did? After all, she had more education in her field of accounting than any of the other women in the company, and her boss relied on her to get the last-minute rush jobs done. She had been wracking her brain trying to figure out what might be at the bottom of her problem—or their problem—but could not come up with any plausible explanations. What was wrong with these women? What was wrong with the boss that he could not see what they were doing to her?

She was truly disturbed about not knowing what to do. It seemed her personal life was going well. She had a good-looking boyfriend who was attentive to her. They had fun whenever they spent time together. They had common interests and both agreed that their careers came before any kind of discussion about the future, including getting married or raising children. Yet, the job situation haunted her to such an extent that her worries spilled over into her relationship with her boyfriend. She was very concerned that the more upset she got about her work situation, the more she became irritable and not emotionally available to her boyfriend, who sensed that she was distant and preoccupied even while

5

they were intimate. She decided that she must get some help, since trying to figure it out on her own for several months had not helped. The approach to the confusing difficulties Elizabeth faced and her effort to understand are quite logical, intuitive, and familiar to all of us. We would do exactly the same in most similar situations. First of all, we want to make sense of what is happening and what might be the meaning of this difficult circumstance. We might say to ourselves, "I have to get to the bottom of this problem," or "I have to understand what is happening to me so that I can fix the problem."

> **TIP FROM THE FIELD**
> Changing one word can make a difference. Replace *why* questions with a *How?* or a curious *How come?*; you will instantly become focused on solutions.

Logical enough. After all, we would do the same when a toaster or a car does not work. In a mechanical problem, all we need to do is find out what is at the bottom of this problem and then we will know what to do to fix it. This way of understanding the cause of the problem and then fixing it is often described as a problem-solving paradigm but is also called a modern or structural view.[*]

Human relationships are much more fluid and unpredictable than a mechanical problem.

Before we dive into the coaching strategies and necessary skills to move toward client goals, perhaps it

---

[*] DeJong, P., & Berg, I. K. (2002). *Interviewing for solutions* (2nd ed.). Pacific Grove, CA: Brooks/Cole.

would be helpful to pause to examine where brief coaching came from and why this approach makes sense for the coaching field.

THE ORIGIN OF BRIEF COACHING

Unlike the traditional therapeutic approach, the group of people who came together joining Steve de Shazer and Insoo Kim Berg in Milwaukee were driven to find something effective and efficient, meaning it would work well to satisfy clients and would not take a long time to find or create solutions. Because they were a group of clinicians in a clinical setting, and not in academia, they began to experiment with what might work, not on what caused the problem. Having been influenced by the work of the Mental Research Institute of Palo Alto[*] on cybernetics and communications theory,[†] the group experimented with their brief therapy model and began seeing clients, hundred and hundreds of clients, from all walks of life. They deliberately did not screen out any particular cases but accepted whoever was sent or walked through the door with real or imagined life problems.

---

[*] Weakland, J., Fisch, R., Watzlawick, P., & Bodin, A. (1974). Brief therapy: Focused problem resolution. *Family Process, 13,* 141–168.

[†] Watzlawick, P., Beavin, J., & Jackson, D. D. (1967). *Pragmatics of human communication.* New York: Norton.

The Milwaukee group was very much interested in what worked, not in what the problems were that interfered with people moving on with their lives. They were not interested in what did not work, or what was lacking in people, but instead looked for ways that people found solutions. The model developed inductively; that is, it did not begin with a theory but through an inductive process to see what worked and did not work, rather than how it should work. The learning curve was very steep when they threw out the theory and even decided on a "theory of no theory." In the process, the team kept observing and learning, focusing on observation of what worked. Along the way, they recognized that language played a key role in the change process. That is, language is the most important tool in relationships and making desired changes.

Language is not only an expression of what we are thinking about. Through talking and listening, activities that use words, we humans also formulate and create new ideas and make changes.[*] When there is no word for an idea, we cannot discuss the concept the word might represent. At the same time, we can create new ideas and images through the use of words as well.

The team discovered that the more clients talked about what they wanted to do, the more animated and

---

[*] Gergen, K. J. (1985). The social constructionist movement in American psychology. *American Psychology, 40*, 266–275. McNamee, S., & Gergen, K. J. (Eds.). (1992). *Therapy as social construction*. Newbury Park, CA: Sage.

excited clients became. The more they described how upset and overwhelmed they were by the burdens of their jobs, for example, the more they became depressed and felt like life was out of control. The team discovered that the more clients talked about hopeful things they wanted in their future, the more hopeful they became. Furthermore, the longer they talked about this hopeful future in greater detail, the more animated, excited, and creative they became. Of course, the opposite is also true. Furman and Ahola called this *solution talk* and *problem talk*.[*]

MAJOR TENETS OF THE SOLUTION-BUILDING PARADIGM

So how do people change through coaching? Change, from being uncertain and having doubts about oneself to becoming confident enough to make personal and situational changes, all occurs through talking first. Of course, behavioral changes must occur as well. Talking first lays out what the finished picture of being more confident might be like, and then clients can implement the pictures they painted with the coach through talking back and forth. Talking involves rather complex skills and requires ever-changing strategies and moment-to-moment decisions and tactics to emphasize a specific topic but minimize other topics that may not contribute to generating

---

[*] Furman, B., & Ahola, T. (1992). S*olution talk: Hosting therapeutic conversation.* New York: Norton.

solutions. How we use inflections and tone of voice can make the same word mean something with an entirely different twist or meaning. How long we talk about one topic but not about other topics, how much emotional intensity we allow on one topic but not others, all influence the meaning of a conversation. It is also true that a listener has as much influence on the nature of conversation as the speaker does.

READER'S EXPERIMENT

Apply this rule to your coaching: Find out what you are doing in your practice that works for you, such as allowing yourself 10 minutes between sessions or going outside to get fresh air twice a day. We are sure you will notice many things that you do well. Doing more of what works in your practice is a very good start for a successful coaching business.

Because this moment-to-moment selection process during coaching conversation moves so quickly, it is important that all coaches have a clear foundation of belief and clear sense of what their roles are because they can be expressed without our awareness. In addition, we are not very good at masking, hiding, or pretending to believe in something when we do not. Therefore, it is important to take some time out to spell out what coaching activities are and some basic assumptions we have about the tasks at hand.

The following is the list of assumptions developed by the Milwaukee group that shaped their work and the discovery of innovative techniques based on common sense and a pragmatic view of what works.

If it works, don't fix it. The most important rule is to find out what works, even a little bit and even once in a while. The second part of this rule is not to fix something that already works. This means that if the client does not complain about something that a coach might see as problematic, it is advised not to make it a problem. True to the rule of staying on the surface of the problem, for example, Elizabeth related that she and her boyfriend, Bill, are a perfect match right now. It does not mean that the relationship will stay perfect for the rest of her life, but for now, she does not say it is broken and needs fixing.

This rule means we are respectful enough to accept her view that other parts of her life are working well and do not need to be fixed. The only thing that is broken for her and that she needs help with is her relationship with her coworkers. It would be a serious mistake for a coach to assume that he or she knows better than the client and look into Elizabeth's relationship with Bill. It would be a grave mistake to pursue a pathway to a problem that the client does not see and even try to persuade the client to accept it as a potential source of a problem.

If something worked once, do more of it. Whatever you are doing or the client is doing, if you learn that it worked even once, find a way to repeat it. For example, Elizabeth found that when she sits down at her desk and looks at the list of tasks at hand and the pile of work awaiting, she can forget about her coworkers and do a good job. So it is important to find all the minute details of what Elizabeth does to concentrate on her work and get her to repeat this over and over so that her productive time becomes longer and longer.

This rule can apply to coaching very nicely. Find out what you are doing in your practice that works for you, such as allowing yourself 10 minutes between sessions or going outside to get fresh air twice a day, and numerous other things you do. We are sure you will notice many things that you do as well as what your clients are doing that work. Getting them to repeat these solutions is a very good start for successful coaching because it not only empowers clients, but also offers an alternative view to how they feel now, that is, that their lives are not going well.

If it does not work, do something different. How can you tell whether you or your client are doing something that is not working and it is time to do something different? If you find yourself saying to yourself, or if you hear your clients telling you with desperation in their voices, "I've tried everything I can think of and nothing works!" or "I feel like I am spinning my wheels," or "I can't take this one more day!" or "I am at the end of my rope," it usually means you or your clients have reached a point of feeling like you have tried everything under the sun. Then, indeed, take yourself and your client seriously enough to stop doing what you have been doing and take a breath. It is time to do something different.

Do you know what *not* to do? Knowing what not to do is just as important as knowing what to do. When we mention this to clients, their usual response is, "Do what? What should I do differently?" Not so fast. First we need to take a deep breath and find out what it is that clients have been doing that they should not repeat because it does not work. There are predictable patterns to human interactions. Therefore, find out what clients have been doing that seems to produce a predictable outcome. Later we will talk more about what to do instead of doing the same thing that will cause the same predictable results. Doing something different means something very different, and this requires thinking outside the box. We cover this more fully in Chapter 4 when we discuss working with challenging situations.

Change is constant and inevitable. Unlike the view that life is stable and predictable, when we look at a very small unit of our lives, change is constant and everywhere. Most people wish for stability and predictability, but life is full of changes. No two days are exactly alike because today we are not exactly the same people that we were yesterday. Perhaps we learned something that we did not know yesterday, and maybe tomorrow we will have a new experience that is slightly different from today. As the famous saying goes, "We can never step into the same river twice."

So how can we coaches take advantage of this reality of life? We can look for small changes clients have already made on their own before they came to see us, for example. They may or may not be aware of this small change, but they certainly know a little more about their situations than they did yesterday. For many clients, picking up the telephone to set up an appointment with you is already a change for them: They have started doing something different about whatever was frustrating to them.

If we truly believe that change is inevitable, then it has important implications for our work. Since clients will change anyway, whether positively or in a negative direction, our task becomes helping clients to be on the lookout for positive changes so that they can continue in that direction. We will describe in more detail how to do this in chapter two.

The future is negotiated and created. Regardless of where the person has been, it is more important to learn what the person wants to do about today and tomorrow. Many people believe that if someone has a criminal background, even though it might be a minor violation of the law, then that person will always be a criminal. It is important that you believe that all clients can change, even though their past may not have been happy or rosy. We human beings are not slaves to our past. We can and do make choices and decisions about how to shape our future, even with seriously difficult past history. At the same time, what we are today is not always the result of what happened to us yesterday. Therefore, the task of coaching is to continuously search for ways to make the most of what the client has and to maximize positive effects wherever we can find and create them.

Small solutions can lead to large changes. The common belief is that a big, serious, and complex problem requires a massive amount of change over a long time. This kind of belief can paralyze the coach and client, leaving them feeling helpless and overwhelmed. Remember the small snowball rolling down the hill? All you have to do is to stay out of its way because the longer and farther it rolls down the hill, the stronger and bigger it becomes. Often the aim of brief coaching is to get the initial small snowball rolling down the hill, while knowing how to stay out of its path as it becomes bigger and bigger. That is, you should avoid interfering with its progress. Sometimes it might take time or detour from a straight and narrow path, but it will eventually reach the goal.

Problems and solutions may not always be directly related. This concept may be shocking and counterintuitive for many coaches. It is surprising to us as well, even after more than 20 years of working with this approach. It goes against all the intuition and knowledge we have gained over the years. According to the problem-solving paradigm, there should be a logical and coherent connection between problems and solutions. Of course, this is true often enough. However, in many situations this thinking does not hold. Too many exceptions call for a closer look and should not be dismissed. As we show later with case examples, when repeated attempts at solutions do not work, it is a very good idea to think of doing something very different, even something absurd and off-the-wall. A crazy thing may somehow have a better chance of working than those logical and reasonable solutions that result in the same frustration and hopelessness. All we can think is that perhaps human logic is not as foolproof as we are led to believe.

No problem happens all the time. Discovery of this fact in the early 1980s was a surprise to the Milwaukee team. For example, Elizabeth had no difficulty concentrating on her work as soon as she sat down at her desk, even forgetting about her troubles for a long time while she focused on her work. Our initial reaction was to be surprised at this. We quickly learned that many such exceptions happen to most clients. For example, if she has such difficulty getting along with her coworkers, how is it that she has a wonderful boyfriend who thinks the world of her? How is it that her boss has such high regard for her work that he increased her responsibility?

We learned that exceptions could be related to different locations, roles, tasks, or people, or even a different time of the week. How is it that even the people who are most difficult at the office can have good friends from their childhood days or in the neighborhood, for example? Many couples who just do not seem to get along with each other often report that when they are out socially with another couple they both like, they have no problem between themselves as well as with their friends. A person who seems difficult can be a wonderful friend to others in other social contexts.

Ask questions rather than telling clients what to do. Questions are an important communication element in all models of coaching, but in brief coaching we view questions as the primary tool of communication and rarely make direct challenges or confrontations to a client. However, questions are both the primary communication method and an intervention.

Give compliments. Compliments are an essential part of the solution-building approach. Validating what clients are already doing well, and acknowledging how difficult their problems are, encourages clients to change while giving the message of the coach's understanding and concern. Compliments in conversation can punctuate what the client is doing right.

Gently nudge to do more of what is working. Once the coach has created a positive and understanding atmosphere through compliments and positive engagement, along with discovery of exceptions to problems, a coach can gently nudge clients to do more of what has

> **TIP FROM THE FIELD**
>
> Utilize Change. Our task as coaches is to make use of changes that clients have managed to create in the most positive way possible.

previously worked, to try changes clients have thought they might like to try. Because these suggestions are based on their own experience and ideas, clients are much more likely to invest in trying out the ideas and using what has worked in the past.

HOW PEOPLE CHANGE

Coaching is about making changes in both perceptions and behaviors. Elizabeth wants herself to change from being a victim of what she believes her coworkers are doing to her to becoming more comfortable with them. Since it is all about changing people, we need to think a little bit about how changes happen. Many people, like Elizabeth, want to understand their problem, even though we know that understanding alone is not enough to cause change. There has to be some sort of outward indication in form of different observable behavior.

Many people believe that a person changes from the inside out, that is, some sort of internal changes occur in thoughts and feelings, and then behavioral changes will follow. It may be true. At the same time, it also may be true that outward changes can create internal changes. As they say, you can "fake it until you make it." Our language is organized in a similar way. Accepting both views makes it possible for us to become much more flexible so that we can work with clients who are oriented toward internal change or external change. Most clients like Elizabeth, although introspective, want action immediately. Sometimes action comes first, and then insight or understanding follows. I am sure you have had this kind of experience in your own life. For example, until we talked about it, Elizabeth did not realize that once she gets to her desk and plunges into her work, she does a fine job of focusing on her work, even forgetting about her troubles with her coworkers.

Therefore, while we talk about mind-body connections, we increasingly accept body-mind interactions as well. It is the duality of both/and that we would like to emphasize here. If only a single, linear view of change is accepted, then we may have to wait a long time for changes to occur for those who operate differently than we do. Behavioral changes can cause feelings to change, while changes in feelings can also lead to behavioral changes. Changes in perception and cognition can also lead to changes in feelings and behaviors, and so it goes. Being able to work with the duality of how human beings function makes us more flexible, thus being able to reach many more clients. Once a person makes a small change, then everything tends to look different from this changed perspective.

Assumptions About People

Everything we do automatically and intuitively is based on years of training and habitual experience that tells us we can reasonably expect certain things to happen. Therefore, we have become accustomed to assuming that traffic lights will work, seasonal changes are predictable, and we can rely on our friends to be supportive, until change shocks us and we realize that life is not always so predictable.

It is useful to be reminded about some of the underlying beliefs related to our work and clearly understand what kind of attitudes we hold toward our clients, because our basic attitudes are very transparent and we are not, as a group in general, very good at pretending or masking our attitudes toward certain things or people. When we are faced with difficult and unclear circumstances we have never faced before, we are guided by our principles and not by emotions alone. What may seem obvious to the client can at times be murky and unclear, and these guidelines and assumptions also indicate to us how to phrase certain questions as well as how to respond in a helpful way even in unfamiliar circumstances. We believe that the following ideas are the foundation of the profession of coaching. When a coach embraces these assumptions about clients, it makes it easier to listen for their good intentions behind what could be considered unacceptable behaviors and thoughts. Thus, it helps us engage with clients quickly and effectively. Look at the following list carefully and study whether you agree with the items or not. If not, you might want to think about how would you change the following items.

Until proven otherwise, we believe that all clients:

- Are doing the best they can under very difficult circumstances
- Are invested in ideas they generate
- Want to do be ethical, courteous, polite, and honest and want to improve their lives
- Want to get along with others such as clients and colleagues
- Want to be accepted and belong to a group
- Want to make their lives better as well as the lives of those they love, respect, and admire
- Want to take care of important others and be taken care of by them
- Want to leave a positive legacy and make a positive difference in the world
- Want to be respected by others and to respect others

WHAT TO SAY AND HOW TO SAY IT

Clients seek your help for a variety of reasons and of course they have a variety of ideas of what might happen. You certainly have no control over what clients may have heard about coaching or about you from your referral sources, just as you have no control over their expectations of what it might do for them. Therefore, it is a good idea to find out by asking, "How did you find your way to my office?" Some clients who are very literal might say, "I drove over here," or, as one client replied, "I took the number 23 bus." You may want to get the paperwork out of the way before you begin the session, and again, there are a number of different ways to do it. Some coaches prefer to mail the initial intake information form to the client before the first session, along with a simple brochure on what to expect, the fee, the coach's credentials, and how to find the office.

It is reasonable to think that the client has already initiated the change process by making a telephone call. For example, instead of suffering each morning's agony and stress over the unpredictable nature of her day at the office, Elizabeth's picking up the phone and arranging an appointment can be viewed as her initiation of change. Rather than doing the same thing over and over as she had done for 6 months, Elizabeth decided to do something about the unbearable situation. Picking up the phone was her way of breaking the repetitive pattern of feeling like a victim and an effort to take control over her life at the office. Viewed this way, her decision to make the phone call was her first step toward what could be a significant change in her life at the office.

Socializing

It is a good idea to spend a few minutes just getting to know the client and there are many ways to do so. Some clients, under a great deal of pressure, may not like small talk, and will be anxious to get going with the task at hand. You can adapt yourself to the client's needs because you can always come back to whatever missing information you need at the end of the session.

Even though it may seem like small talk and a waste of time, you can get a great deal of information about the client by simply asking what kind of work he or she does. "How long have you done this kind of work?" "Wow, sounds like it is a very technical job. You must have worked very hard to get into this kind of work." Thus you allow clients an opportunity to self-compliment as they respond to your comment. Asking questions this way also gives you an opportunity to acknowledge their successes and

> **QUESTION FROM THE FIELD**
>
> "What about underlying causes? You do not seem to pay much attention to them."
>
> In our view, underlying causes may exist for many behaviors. However, often they do not prevent more useful behavior from happening. We have found that when clients manage to do things that are helpful in reaching their goals, most of the underlying problems are no longer a concern.

accomplishments in life. This signals to clients that you are interested not only in their difficulties, but also in getting the larger picture of their lives.

A simple question that you can follow up with might be something like "Are you good at what you do?" which immediately establishes the client's competence and experience. Another question, "Does your boss think you do a good job?," provides you with information about the client's job situation and about how others close to the client might view him or her. This allows room to find out whether the client agrees or disagrees with the boss's evaluation of his or her competence, for example.

You can also easily start a session by asking, as Steve de Shazer does, "How do you spend your time?" This simple, straightforward question can generate all sorts of useful information about the client immediately. Clients may indicate that they do not have enough time and this is part of the stress, or they have too much time on their hands. Still others respond by detailing their daily routine, thus giving you an overall picture of what their lives are like.

Changing Complaints Into a Goal Negotiation

All client complaints are useful to listen to because they tell you how the client thinks about what is not working in his or her life, and thus, what needs to be changed. On the other hand, dwelling on complaints and problems too long makes it difficult to change the focus of the conversation to a useful dialogue about the outcome of coaching that the client is looking for. All complaints or problems contain a seed of solution, depending on how you choose to respond to it.

Consider the following dialogue:

Elizabeth: I am really upset about what is happening in my job.
Coach: I see. You would like to find some solution to your job problem.

Imagine if the coach's response was, "Tell me more about what is bothering you about your job." You can easily imagine what kind of conversation might follow next: a great deal of problem talk, even before you know what it is that the client wants to find solutions for. Therefore, how we phrase the question can be heard as an invitation to extend the problem talk or an invitation to tell us about how the coaching session would fit into the client's overall life situation and how much distress the problem causes them. Listen to how a coach can redirect the conversation into something more focused on solutions.

Elizabeth: Yeah, it's been really bothering me so much that I dread going to work and facing my coworkers.
Coach: So, it sounds like what you would like to find out is how to get along with your coworkers.
Elizabeth: I am not sure if there is hope for them, but I want to make sure that I don't get so upset with them that I may jeopardize my job. I want to keep my job.

Coach: Of course. It sounds like keeping your job is important to you, as well as getting along with your coworkers.

Elizabeth: I am not sure if it is possible but I sure would like to try and find out if I can do both.

Observe how the client provides more and more useful information about what is important to her as the conversation continues.

Finding Out What Is Important to the Client

In relatively few exchanges, a coach can quickly come to find out what is important to the client because this is where the client's energy is and this is what the client is invested in changing. When we follow what is important to clients, it means they are more likely to be invested in making necessary changes to achieve their goals. As we all know, everybody is interested in carrying out their own ideas for solutions, rather than blindly following someone else's ideas. The steps they take must make sense to them before they are willing to invest their time and energy to make the necessary changes. Therefore, when clients propose the necessary steps they need to take, they are more likely to own the outcome with pride and a sense of accomplishment.

At the same time, it also is important to help clients create their own map of how they are going to implement their own ideas. During supervision, consultations, and workshops we conduct, we frequently hear the participant coaches saying things like, "I am really frustrated. I listened very carefully to what was important to Gary and he said he was going to make the necessary changes, but he has not done anything!" If this is your mumbling about someone like Gary, stop blaming the client and carefully review and find out whether you have helped Gary to create his own map for how he will implement his good intentions. A detailed map is what the client often needs. Because the client is the expert on his or her life, deciding where to turn left or which landmarks will tell him that he is coming close to his destination will be the client's task. At the same time, the coach's expertise is in how to create a map. We show more about how to develop this expertise.

Finding Out Who Is Important to the Client

Along with what is important to the client, learning who is important to the client is a helpful resource. For example, for someone other than Elizabeth, having a good relationship with her boyfriend may be enough. For Elizabeth, however, getting along well socially and maintaining friendly relationships with her female coworkers is particularly important. When we learn how important this is to her, then we can focus immediately on this desire, listening intently to her to understand who is important. The next step we can take, then, is to find out what kind of positive difference this will make to her. Instead of assuming we know what it means to get along with her coworkers, our next task is to ask many detailed questions about how she will know that she is getting along with other people and what will change with herself.

Such simple and commonly used words as "getting along with others" may mean many different things to different people. For example, for some, it may mean they say good morning with a smile in the morning, then say good-bye with a smile at the end of the day. In other words, a lack of any overt conflict may be very important to one person, but a different sort of getting along may be important to another. We must ask Elizabeth, "What will be going on with you and your coworkers that will tell you that you are getting along enough so that you can feel comfortable and relaxed about coming to work?" "What will you see them do that they are not doing right now that will tell you that you are getting along with them?" When you are this specific, then you can be sure that Elizabeth knows what she is looking for as an indication that she and her coworkers are getting along. Otherwise, somewhere along the way, we may learn about what is important to her, but we cannot be sure without asking.

To be clear which is more important to her, to keep the job or to get along with her coworkers, we can always find out by asking her to help us learn more from her so that we can help her figure out what the solution might be. Listen to the following dialogue.

Coach: Which would you say is more important to you, to keep the job or to get along with your coworkers?

Elizabeth: Definitely keeping my job. Of all the jobs I have had, this is the best one. My boss gives me lots of responsibility and lets me make decisions on my own without micromanaging me, like the other ones I have had.

Coach: I see you really like challenges, making decisions, and knowing that you are doing a good job.

Elizabeth: Oh, yes. This is the first time I have a boss who really trusts me. That's why it is important to me to keep up with my work and stay productive.

Now it is becoming a bit more clear what is important to Elizabeth, that is, not only to keep her job but also to maintain her autonomy and face challenges such as making her own decisions and taking responsibility for her decisions. Now we are learning a little bit more about Elizabeth.

CLARITY OF CLIENT GOALS

It is not uncommon that clients as articulate and well-educated as Elizabeth do not walk into a coaching session with a clear sense of what their desired outcomes are. If it were so clear, they probably would not need us because they would already know what to do. Therefore, it is worthwhile to spend a considerable amount of time negotiating the goal before we jump into the coaching process. Our experience is that even the most bright, smart, highly motivated, and educated clients often need a great deal of help to clarify the signs that their goals are being achieved. When it is painful or uncomfortable, of course, the natural response is to look for a quick solution to whatever is causing them enough concern that they want to seek outside help.

> **TIP FROM THE FIELD**
>
> Clarify your fee before the first meeting. Explain that your coaching will begin with the first session and so will your fee. Offer to allow clients to pay for the first session when they have found it useful.

Listen to the following conversation about being clear about the presence of solutions rather than an absence of problems.

Coach: So what is your best hope for this meeting? What needs to come out of this meeting today so that you can say that it has been useful for you to take the time to come and talk to me?

Client: I am not sure what to say when you put it that way. I just know I am really stressed out with so many things going on in my life. I just need some peace, I guess. It's been a tough year. My productivity has gone down and I am not accomplishing as much as I would like to.

Coach: So what needs to be changed first so that you can say that at least you are beginning to see the light at the end of the tunnel?

Client: That's a good analogy. I feel like I've been traveling in the dark tunnel for such a long time and I don't feel like I am accomplishing anything.

Coach: So what you would like is to feel more productive, feel like you are accomplishing something.

Client: That's it. I need to feel like I am accomplishing something productive, you know.

Coach: So let's just suppose you do feel you are accomplishing something. I am not sure yet how you will get there, but somehow you reach a place where you feel like you are accomplishing something. What will tell you that you are productive?

Client: Oh, that's easy. I will feel like getting up in the morning. My morning routine will have a purpose, like I am eager to get to the office and really stay focused on my work. I will not waste time fussing about my coffee or check my e-mails all the time and just chitchat with old buddies.

Coach: Of course. So what would you do instead?

Client: I will stick to my task of doing the research, even though it's boring. I'll find some interesting pattern in the banking system that may tell me a new trend in how customers use online banking and how to encourage them to use more online banking. I know I am creative, but I need to get back to having creative juices flowing.

As you can see, it is important for the coach to be gently persistent with the search for what the client would consider a successful outcome. Again, we like to emphasize that brief coaching is a very goal-driven activity, and knowing the outcome of the useful conversation between the coach and the client is the essential ingredient.

Changing Goals in Midstream

We are asked about changing goals from time to time by trainees who seem confused about what to do when clients change their minds and come up with new goals. It is not surprising, and it occurs even with experienced coaches as well.

One client explained it this way: "You know, when I started talking to you, the issue of job security with this company was uppermost in my mind and now that it is settled, I realize that I did not even see that I was not feeling productive and creative in my work. So now I need to address this issue." This is a perfectly natural outcome. The next step is to start over with a fresh negotiation of the client's goal. Job security is a rather concrete goal that depends a great deal on someone giving reassurances that the client will either keep the job or will have to leave. It is easy to determine whether such a concrete goal has been achieved.

However, such goals as "being more creative" or "feeling more productive" are much more vague and related to internal states, rather than to outward measurable and concrete achievements. Therefore it is necessary for the coach to begin the goal negotiation steps again, but with a small difference: The coach must define some outward signs of what "creative juices flowing" might look like, such as other people noticing the client's creativity or some other outward sign that is visible to important people around the client. Again, taking some time in the beginning to negotiate the detailed description of achieving goals might sound like the following:

Coach: Suppose you become more creative. How could you tell that you are becoming more creative?

Client: Because I would be eager to go to work. I would be excited and concentrate on what I am doing and not get so distracted. I would want to experiment with many different ideas and I'd be excited about having so many ideas, and not feel like it's a burden.

Coach: So suppose you become so excited about having so many ideas. What would your coworkers see you doing differently that would tell them that your creative juices are flowing?

Client: Some of my coworkers have seen me this way before. I become quiet, very concentrated and focused. They know enough to leave me alone and not bother me because I often don't even hear them when they talk to me. Then they will know I am onto something very exciting and creative. When I get distracted, I easily lose my focus and I go around bothering other people. Some even get irritated with me.

When the outcome of the coaching session is clear, most clients are competent to figure out what steps they need to take to arrive at the desired state. It is also important for the coach to realize when and under what circumstances the client's effort has not paid off in the way that he or she had hoped. Therefore the coach should not recommend or suggest that the client repeat the same mistakes. A simple question like, "So, how well did it work? I mean, your getting all upset and annoyed with what others are doing?" The answers would give you ample clues on what not to recommend.

Therefore, quickly assessing what and who is important to the client is the first important information that will tell a coach how to frame what the client needs to do differently. When the client feels his or her point of view is respected, accepted, and explained, the working relationship between the coach and the client can develop rather quickly.

In the following section, we return to the story of Elizabeth and discuss the details of solutions that tell the client and the coach the landmark signs that will show them that they have arrived at their destination and that they can get off the train.

CREATING A DETAILED ROAD MAP

As we indicated earlier, the road map of coaching should not only show clients how and where to begin a journey through many conversations but also tell them where to get off the road and that they have arrived at their destination. We now return to the road map that Elizabeth needs to know that she and the coach have successfully completed their trip to her destination. We think the best way to describe the method of mapping out her journey is to show you by listening to their conversation.

Coach: I would like to get back to what you said earlier. You mentioned that you would like to keep the job and also get along with your coworkers at the same time.

Elizabeth: Yes, I want both. That's not much to ask for and I think I can have both. Well, I should.

Coach: So let's just suppose you can have both. Sounds like you already have one of the two: You already have the job and your boss gives you more responsibility and more autonomy, and he thinks you are doing a good job.

Elizabeth: I am quite confident about that part. Only if you can help me with the second part . . . but that's where I am stuck.

Coach: Yes, it seems that way. So, let's just imagine this problem with your coworkers is solved somehow. We don't know how yet, but somehow the problem is solved. How will you know that, "Hey, I am getting along with my coworkers!" How would you be able to say that? What will you see so that you can say that to yourself?"

Elizabeth: As I said before, I just want them to be friendly to me. I don't expect them to love me, but just be social, make small talk once in a while, and maybe even have lunch together or carry on some girl talk, you know.

Coach: Of course these things are important and help to maintain a good office atmosphere.

Elizabeth: Yes, that's what I want. I am a social person and I don't want to be treated like I have some kind of infectious disease or something like that.

Coach: So, suppose you have the kind of relationship you want with your coworkers. What difference would it make to you?

Engaging the client's imagination related to the details of the solution is a crucial beginning step. Elizabeth still is very much focused on what is missing in her life rather than what she wants to replace it with. In other words, a concrete indication of the presence of solutions is the exact details of the road map that she will need to make the necessary changes. Notice how useful it is to get the client to imagine the solution.

Elizabeth: Well, I certainly want to know that I can get along with anybody and that's important to me because I want someday to move up to something higher than an accountant. I am ambitious. I agree with my boyfriend about that, and someday I want to be in a management position.

Coach: I see. Yes, I can see that you are ambitious and of course it would help you to know that you can manage difficult workers also, and you want to build a good reputation in the company.

Elizabeth: I am not telling this to my boss yet, but I want to build a good career path in this company and to do that, I need to get a good start with coworkers so that my boss will hear good things about me, that I am a nice person to work with, that they all like me.

Coach: I can see that it is very important to you that you build a good foundation for future promotions.

Elizabeth: Yes, of course. Yes, I do.

The motivation and explanation behind the client's unhappiness and her desire to change her relationships with her coworkers now become quite clear. Therefore, what seems to be a rather minor question could shed a great deal of light on what the client considers important. "So what difference would it make for you?" or "How would that be helpful for you, I mean, to have your coworkers become more friendly and social with you?" These simple questions can shed much light, quickly and efficiently, and they are often described as a simple yet economical way to obtain a great deal of useful information.

Now that we know the motivation behind what the client wants, it is time to help her create her own road map to get there as effectively and efficiently as possible.

Coach: So, what is the first small change you need to see with your coworkers that tells you that you are moving in the right direction?

Elizabeth: As I said, I want them to be friendly with me, say good morning to me, have pleasant conversations, and be friendly enough so that they will find out that I am a good person and they can trust me.

Coach: Makes sense. Suppose you have the kind of relationship you are describing. What would your coworkers say you would do then that you are not doing right now?

Notice that this is the second time the coach has used the technique of inviting the client to use her imagination to create an ideal situation that she does not have now, but wishes to have. The question that begins with "Suppose" has a way of turning the complaint into a possible solution because we believe that the client's imagination of realistic solutions is the most important asset that clients do not recognize they have. The first useful idea that all the other women coworkers became friendly with her, and to wonder what Elizabeth would be doing that she is not doing now. More discussion of this type of question follows in Chapter 2 in the section on useful language skills.

> **TIP FROM THE FIELD**
>
> In order to capture presession change: During a presession telephone call, ask clients to keep track of what is happening in their lives that they want to continue. During the first meeting, be sure to find out about the details of those things that are worth continuing.

Utilizing someone else's view is called a relationship question, and this is particularly useful in coaching situations because we pay a great deal of attention to the client's work environment. Most coaching cases are situated in the work environment. What one person does or does not do could have a tremendous impact on the atmosphere, culture, and cohesiveness of the workplace. We influence each other as we interact with each other.

Elizabeth: (*long pause*) Oh, I've never thought about that. . . . That's a good
    question. . . . I suppose they will say that I will smile more in the morn-
    ing, start small talk, be more approachable, a little bit lighter, maybe even
    tell funny stories about a mistake I made and not be so serious all the
    time. I think I just have my nose to the grindstone all the time at work.
    They might even say that I am not that much fun to be around.
Coach: Suppose you keep this up a while, being lighter, telling funny things
    about yourself, and lowering your guard a little bit more. What would
    they say they would do then that they are not doing right now?
Elizabeth: They would say I am easier to approach, more relaxed, and not
    so serious all the time. I suppose it will make it easier for them to be
    friendly with me.

We know that we cannot change other people, especially those who do not see the need for change. Yet we
frequently come across clients who want us to change
other people for them, an impossible task, because it
seems quite clear that Elizabeth's coworkers are quite
content to get along with each other. The person who is
most anxious to change this is Elizabeth, not her
coworkers. Therefore, it is important for the coach to
assess how realistic the client's goals are. If you decide
that it is not a realistic goal because we cannot change
other people, then you will need to redirect the client's
attention or use a new relationship question. Clearly
what needs to be changed here is the relationship
Elizabeth has with her coworkers, and now we understand her ambition to move up in the organization.

Therefore, helping Elizabeth to imagine what her coworkers will see changed about her will greatly influence their attitudes toward her. This is the best way to get to where she wants to go.

USING THE CLIENT'S SKILLS

Now that we know where Elizabeth wants to go, the next information we need is: Does she know how to be friendly and sociable, how to carry on small talk, and how to be relaxed with others and not so serious all the time? When the client knows how to be relaxed, sociable, friendly, and easy to talk to, it will be much easier to repeat her successful strategies. It takes much hard work for a client to do something he or she does not know how to do. For example, if Elizabeth did not know how to drive a car, we probably would not recommend that she get an expensive and elaborate GPS (global positioning system) for her car. Even when we know what the client's destination is, we want to make sure that the client has all the equipment and skills to navigate the map. Therefore, we need to find out whether Elizabeth actually knows how to smile, be approachable, be relaxed and have fun at all even if in the beginning it is only to carry on small talk with those she feels comfortable with.

We heard in the beginning of the session that she has no difficulty having fun with her boyfriend and is quite comfortable and can even tell funny stories or laugh at her mistakes. But we need to know more about this, as the following conversation shows.

Coach: Suppose I ask your boyfriend or your women friends, what is Elizabeth like when she is relaxed, not so serious, and cheerful? What would they tell me about you?

Elizabeth: Oh, they would tell you that I can be quite fun to be around. I am not so serious all the time, especially around good friends and my boyfriend. We goof around a lot and giggle and joke a lot. I used to be something of a flake in college and I was not very serious about studying but now that I found a job I really like, I find that I am very good at what I do. I think maybe I became so serious all of a sudden. Maybe I'm too serious on the job because I am determined to be successful at my work. This is the first time in my life that I have a definite professional goal and I earn a reasonably good income. Maybe I became just too serious and too focused on my goal. I guess I sort of tend to do that, like cramming for exams all night long for days, without much sleep and not eating much either.

Being an intelligent and bright person, Elizabeth recognizes that she may have contributed to her own problem, that is, because she was too focused on her ambitious goals, she forgot to pay attention to her coworkers as people. They may need some indication from her that she is approachable and that it is safe for them to do so. It means she recognizes that she may have to change first, rather than waiting for the coworkers to change first. The next task for the coach, then, is to help Elizabeth make a more detailed map of how she will use her existing skills to get to the first small success.

Coach: So what might be the first small thing you might do to let your coworkers know that you are approachable, sociable, and not so serious all the time?

Elizabeth: I suppose I will have to break the ice first. I should have known this before, but you know, I have never thought about this until now. They worked together for a few years before I got the job and I think this is the first time this company hired a woman accountant. I am pretty sure that I was so determined to do a good job, I must have really not reached out to them as coworkers. I guess I saw myself as a pioneer or something, you know, being the first woman accountant, and maybe it added to my seriousness. Actually, I am the new kid on the block, and I need them more than they need me. They are friends with each other already and I am the brand new person. Instead of being so serious and working all the time, I should start with small talk and be more friendly with them.

Coach: Sounds like an excellent idea. So what would you do tomorrow morning that you didn't do this morning?

Elizabeth: I am going to bring in some pastries tomorrow morning as a celebration for having survived my first 5 months on the job. Something like that, and ask them how their days are going, instead of waiting for them to ask me.

Coach: Excellent idea.

In this chapter, we laid out some of the basic foundations and assumptions of brief coaching. We hope we have shown you that being effective and efficient can work side by side with a respectful approach to utilizing the abilities and competencies that clients bring with them to the coaching process. It is often the case that many clients have been so preoccupied with their problems that they need a slight nudge from the coach to look in the right direction. In coming chapters, we discuss all the necessary tools to help you deal with more complex situations that will require stepping out of the box, rather than going round and round within the box.

> **TIP FROM THE FIELD**
> Start your coaching conversation asking for a specific goal: "What needs to happen in this coaching session today that will tell you it was worth involving me as your coach?"

CHAPTER TWO

SIMPLE TOOLS FOR SERIOUS TASKS

Obviously, brief coaching is about being brief. What helps make brief coaching brief while maintaining its effectiveness? What influence does being brief have on the coaching conversation, you might ask? In this chapter, we present a great deal of detail on how a first coaching session flows from beginning to end. The reason for emphasizing the first session is that it sets the tone for the coming work and indirectly conveys to clients that the direction of the session is a joint venture. That is, they must take a leading role in deciding where the ending point of the journey will be. At the same time, we emphasize

> **QUESTION FROM THE FIELD**
>
> "What do you tell clients if they ask about the number of sessions necessary?"
>
> First of all, we respect clients' initial judgment of how long they think it will take. We may point out that we are sometimes surprised at how quickly clients manage to get on track. We suggest checking with clients at the end of each session to see whether things have improved enough.

that clients are in the driver's seat from the beginning and they will continue to drive into the sunset following a brief period of guidance from their coaches. The choice of direction will be their own. We hope this book will do the same for you that you will do for your clients. That is, you will set goals and this book will offer useful guidance and suggestions for how to be the best coach for your client, and you will continue the journey of learning and growing as a competent and wise coach.

In each step along the way of this short ride, you and your clients will learn from each other. We hope to show you what makes brief coaching conversation unique. That is, brief coaching is a by-product of a certain kind of conversation, rather than a coaching practice that sets out to be brief. Along the way, we will introduce you to many useful tools that you can take into your practice immediately, even if your practice is not brief.

BEGINNING WITH THE END IN MIND (OR SIGHT)

We would like to begin with an example of a memorable case Peter encountered which taught us both that we can never assume that we know how the case will turn out.

During a workshop on solution-focused coaching I was conducting, a man in his 40s approached me during the morning coffee break and asked whether he could have a few words with me privately. We stepped out on the terrace, making sure of our privacy, and he explained in a hushed voice that he was a journalist in a desperate professional situation. He faced a lawsuit regarding a piece he had written in a newspaper some time before about a well-known person in his city. His professional reputation and career were at stake. Not only that, he could not trust the attorney the management appointed for his defense and was not confident that he could trust the management either. He asked me to keep the conversation confidential and asked if I was willing to accept him as a client because he was at the end of his rope, frightened by the prospect that he might never work as a journalist again anywhere. He felt at a loss for how to handle all the different people he needed to deal with. He wanted to have the first meeting as soon as possible and wanted to be sure I had the time to coach him through the bleak months ahead.

We agreed to hold the first meeting by phone two days later at 10:00 P.M. so that we both would be available to talk a long time if necessary. I explained my fee beginning from the first phone meeting. Since he was participating in the morning session of the workshop, he already knew that I practice brief coaching. I explained that at the end of the first phone conversation, we would decide on the next course of action. I remember worrying about how I would be able to clear my schedule so that I could respond to his urgency during the following weeks, maybe even months.

Upon hearing such a dire story, the first temptation is to find out all about what terrible thing the journalist might have said about the well-known person who was angry enough to sue him. I decided that while it would satisfy my curiosity it would not be terribly helpful to the client, even though I had many other questions, considering my background of practicing law for many years. Of course, my first obligation was to think about what would be helpful to the client. I decided that he knew what kind of mess he was in and I did not need to know the past in order to be helpful to him today and tomorrow.

I set aside these ideas and decided to stay close to the usual brief coaching model. At the beginning of our phone conversation I asked him, "So, what needs to happen here tonight that would tell you it was worth involving me as a coach?" He initially laid out some background information and sketched in his current situation, which was not very comforting for him. His wife, even though she had been very patient and understanding, had begun to suffer from stress and was complaining about his preoccupation. He was distracted and absentminded, neglecting his children much more than he usually did when he worked on serious writing for long hours. On the litigation front, things were dragging and he faced a long, uncertain court case. Finally, answering my initial question, he said that he really needed to sort out the important from the less important, take the legal situation in hand, come up with some realistic options for his professional future, and find the peace and energy to handle one thing at a time.

I promised him that we would come back to all the topics he listed, but before we moved forward, I had a question. "OK, first let's begin with the end in mind. Suppose just for a moment that you have sorted out things, taken matters into your own hands, and somehow found the energy and peace to get through this ordeal. How will you know that things have improved enough to stop meeting like this?"

> **HOT QUOTATION**
>
> "All of the facts belong to the problem, not to the solution."
>
> —*Ludwig Wittgenstein*

There was a long pause. Then he said, "Probably something in the reaction of my wife and children would be a clear sign . . . that I would find my inner balance . . . knowing that I had done everything in my power on one hand, and then on the other hand, letting go of things that I could not change." As he was answering my third repeat of the question, "What else would be different?," something seemed to come over him. Suddenly I could sense that something changed. From his confident tone of voice and the speed of his speech, I knew that we might not need any more sessions after that phone call. Of course, I needed to check it out with him, so I said somewhat hesitantly, "Hearing the things you are saying, I mean, what you are saying and how you are saying it, I wonder, could it be that things are already better enough for you?" He said he was just thinking about the very same thing. He said he felt like he had cold water splashed on his face and what he wanted to do next and his precise ideas on how to do it became so much clearer. He said he sensed "a total U-turn in the whole matter." Then he went on to say, "To be honest, and to my complete surprise, I am confident that I can handle things on my own again. Thank you, coach!"

With a total of no more than 20 minutes, it was definitely the shortest coaching process I have ever conducted. About a year later, I ran into my client by chance. I did not ask and he did not volunteer specific information about the litigation. Yet he made it clear that he had begun to take matters into his own hands and was on the road of success.

Clearly this is an unusual example of how brief a brief coaching session can become when it begins with the end in mind. As we describe in some detail in this chapter, devoting some time to negotiating the desirable outcome of the coaching not only sets the road map but also lets us know when we have arrived at the destination.

GOAL NEGOTIATIONS

Even though we addressed goal negotiation in Chapter 1, we want to remind you again that coming to an agreement about where the finish line will be is the most important tool of brief coaching. When the finish line keeps moving around, coaching can become a long-term endeavor and we may aimlessly meander the country-side without knowing where we are or how far away the finish line is. Even though it sounds simple and easy, actually negotiating how you will know that you can stop meeting takes some effort and time. We believe that knowing the outcome will make this effort productive and efficient, which is no different than other projects in life. In this section we list some useful criteria that will help you to be clear about what you are looking for. We believe all goals must have the following elements to be useful guides.

The Presence of Solutions, Rather Than Absence of Problems

When we begin the process of negotiating goals, many clients list what difficulties or lack of satisfaction will be removed from their lives, rather than what new solution or activities would be there instead. For example, the most common client responses to questions such as, "What needs to happen here so that this session is help-ful to you?" or "What is your best hope for this meet-ing?" are, "I won't have this tense feeling in my stomach when I think about what I could have achieved with my life," "I can't face going to work in the morning any-more," "I won't be so tired all the time," or other similar statements about what difficulties or tension will be gone from their lives or workplace.

Having been a taxi driver during my (Peter's) student days, asking clients where they wanted to go was the most natural thing to do, since my task was to take clients where they wanted to go, not where I thought they should go. If a customer wanted me to take him to a bar, it never occurred to me to take him to his home and wife instead. The same rule applies to coaching. Yet the negotiation of where the client wants to go seems simple enough but is surprisingly difficult. Therefore, during this early negotiation phase, clients need considerable help from their coaches. We want to mention a beautiful teaching strategy of Timothy Gallwey, using a tennis metaphor.

Case Example

During a coaching conference, a well-known coach and former tennis professional, Tim, gave a demonstration on the lesson of goal negotiations. A participant asked Tim to help him with his defensive backhand. He explained that he had suffered for several years with constant backhand volley problems and had taken many tennis lessons from many trainers to get rid of the problem without success. Tim wanted to see for himself what the participant's problem was, so he asked the man to demonstrate his backhand volley problems in front of the audience. Sure enough, his description was accurate, so he knew exactly what he was doing wrong. The moment the ball started moving toward the player's left side, his entire body posture signaled, "Oh, oh, here comes trouble directly toward my weakness." The player would hit with his arm in front of his chest, entire upper body leaning backward, and his face expressing anticipation of a disaster. After watching this form a couple of times, Tim stopped, asked the man to go back to the net, and told him, "Yes, you are right. This is probably the most defensive backhand volley I've ever seen. What I do not know, however, is what you want instead. The man started to tell him. But Tim stopped him in the middle of his explanation, saying, "I am a very visual person and I need to see it." Tim asked the man to go back to his side of the court and just show him how he wanted his backhand play to look in the future. Tim began to throw balls again, checking back each time with the player saying, "Is this what you want?" The man first said no a couple of times, correcting and improving his stroke until he said, "Yes, Tim, more like this one!" He did a series

> **TOOLBOX**
> Questions with the end in mind:
>
> How will you know things have improved enough that you do not need to see me anymore?
>
> How will other people notice that things have become better?
>
> What will be the first small sign to tell you that it's time to continue on your own?

of astonishing backhand volleys, fast, energetic, and the audience around the court broke into applause.

Tim jokingly said to the man, "Well, I see, so that's what you want—too bad you can't do it now." The moment Tim said this the volley goes back to defensive. Tim says, "Exactly that's how you do it, and what would you like instead?" And immediately the volleys change back to powerful strike again.

The presence of a solution is just as important in any coaching conversation as it was in this tennis example. The following is a list of questions you might ask during the goal negotiation phase:

- What needs to happen here today that will tell you that it was a good idea to come to see me today?
- What would your best friend (coworkers, boss) see that will tell him or her that your coming to see me was very helpful to you without your saying it?
- What would you do instead? (e.g., if the client were staying in bed all day unable to get up)
- Would that be a big change or a small change for you?
- Suppose you are able to get your paperwork done on time. What would be different for you?
- Who will be the first person to notice that you are able to get your paperwork done?

- What would this person do then that he or she didn't do this morning?

Many more details of the solution picture are helpful to clients because of the many changes and solutions they discuss with you. Even if they make only one small behavioral change, the chances of causing the ripple effect in other parts of their lives will increase with time. This kind of detailed conversation can take up to 10 to 15 minutes. It is amazing how much can be covered when the conversation is focused only on details of solutions.

Small Steps

When we think about brief coaching, it makes sense to assume that it means making a great many changes in a rather short time. Not so. Only one small change is needed to start the snowball down the hill. As the snowball rolls down the hill, it creates momentum and picks up speed as well as size. Changes are created in small pieces; then nature takes over and the ripple effects are carried into areas of life. As time goes on, the ripple effect keeps spreading.

It makes sense for clients to want to rush into big changes because they have tried many things on their own before deciding that they needed help. It is understandable for them to want to jump into making changes, any changes, just to feel like they are doing something. The same goes for a coach as well. However, when we rush into making a big change, it is likely to be the wrong change or in the wrong direction. It may seem too slow to clients as well as to you. However, make sure that you reassure your clients that going slow will help them to get there faster, because it is likely to be the right kind of change to get them going in the right direction.

Solutions in Social Contexts

Since all concerns and issues are defined in social terms, make sure that solutions you discuss with your clients are also defined in social terms. You can do this by making sure to include other important persons in their lives who would recognize the changes and solutions that clients will generate. The beauty of this way of generating solutions is that those important persons in the client's life will do things naturally to support and enforce your client's new and productive behaviors. Not only would the coach emphasize the relationship issues, but these other important persons would spontaneously reinforce and sup-

> **READER'S EXPERIMENT**
>
> Make a prediction before your next coaching session whether the session will be the final one with that particular client. Carefully observe your client throughout the session. Give yourself one point for each correct prediction.

port the positive changes that your clients will make in coming days, weeks, and months, long after the coaching session is over.

Therefore, we suggest using the following questions to highlight important information and ideas:

- What would your friends say that would show you they could tell that this session has been useful to you today?
- What would your boss do differently when he or she notices that you are more confident about yourself without your saying that?
- Suppose you become more involved in generating new ideas for increased productivity. How would your team members let you know that they appreciate it?
- Suppose they do express their appreciation more openly. What would you do then that you don't normally do?
- Suppose you become more cooperative in meetings. What would your colleagues do in reaction?

Realistic and Measurable Goals

Obviously, goals must be realistically achievable and at the same time measurable. When we first meet a client, it is not clear what the client is able to do to attain his or

her goals. Therefore, carefully listening for such information is helpful. Even when you recognize that your
client is quite competent and has accomplished many
things, it is a good idea to check by simply asking the
client. Another important reality is that the goal achievement must be concrete enough to be measurable or
countable, as the following questions indicate:

- What do you know about yourself that tells you
  that you can come to work on time every day?
- What does your boss know about you that tells
  him or her that you can get such big projects
  done in such a short time, even though this is
  the first for you?
- Knowing yourself as well as you do, exactly
  what is it that you would do to get this big project finished on time?
- Suppose you do your best to earn their trust.
  What would your colleagues do to let you know
  that you have finally proved to them that you
  are trustworthy?
- Tell me again—what would they do differently
  to let you know that they realize that you are
  committed to finishing this project on time?

After you come to an agreement with the client about
tangible indicators that will let the client know that he
or she is moving in the right direction, make sure to

remind yourself of this description of goals and check on it periodically so that you and the client can stay focused on achieving the goals. We will show you how to do this respectfully, without being intrusive.

MIRACLE PICTURES

When some clients are too discouraged or do not have the patience for discussing the details of a successful outcome, another very useful tool you can use is called the miracle question, a powerful tool that generates beginning pictures of solutions. This question was born out of a coach's desperation, not knowing what else to do. In the early 1980s, Insoo was interviewing a mother who was so desperate that she initially thought that suicide might be the only solution left for her. The lady's alcoholic husband was losing jobs every few months. Her four children caused such trouble for teachers that she received phone calls daily from each school, always implying that it was her fault that her children were so out of control and that she ought to do something about their impossible behavior. She held down a job to support the family and she was so worn out that she felt that she could not cope with life anymore.

As usual Insoo began to ask the lady about her idea of what might be the best hope for the session. The lady let out a big sigh and sat there for a few moments, and then finally said slowly, "I don't know if there is any hope for me . . . unless . . . you have a miracle." Out of desperation, Insoo picked up on the client's idea of a miracle, and said, "I don't have a miracle, I'm afraid. But suppose I did. What would be different for you then?" The lady sat there for a few minutes and finally said, "I suppose . . . the first thing would be that I would have hope that I would be able to manage my job more productively, not use up my sick days and vacation days, get a raise because I would be more energetic and enthusiastic about coming to work, instead of dragging myself every morning. My husband would keep his job for a change and not get fired. . . . I would have more energy, maybe have something to smile about . . . and my oldest boy's teacher would call me with good news about him, and . . ." She kept making a long list of things that would change. Insoo sat mesmerized by her list, and the team behind the mirror were also stunned by her long list of good ideas that created her own miracles. The Milwaukee group was so energized by this surprising experience that they began using this question with almost every client who walked through the door. Since then this question has been repeated thousands and thousands of times around the world during the past 25 years in every setting from a corporate boardroom to a prison.

Over the years, we have learned a great deal about how to make this miracle question work better. Through trial and error, experimenting with many different approaches, we discovered what seems to work the best. Pay close attention to how this question is phrased. Getting clients to be ready to imagine a solution while they are preoccupied with what is not going well in their lives means they need some serious help from the coach.

> **METAPHOR OF THE MONKEY**
>
> "Let me help you out of the water, so you'll not suffocate," said the friendly monkey, as he lifted the fish out of the river and carefully placed him on a tree branch. Note: What seems reasonable to the coach is not always helpful to the client.

Coach: I am going to ask you a rather strange question that will require a good dose of imagination. (*pause*) Do you have a good imagination? (*pause*)

Client: Yes, I think so.

Coach: Good. The strange question is this. (*pause*) After we talk, obviously you may have to go back to work and get more work done at the office, but it is not over yet, because you still have to go home and have lots of tasks to do yet, such as taking care of the children, cooking dinner, helping them with their schoolwork, giving them baths, and putting them to bed. (*pause*) Finally it is time for you to go to bed. You get into a comfortable bed and get ready for a restful sleep. During the night, while you are in deep sleep, a miracle strikes your house and the result is that all the worries and anxieties that brought you here to talk to me are all gone, just like that (*snapping fingers*). Because this happens during the night when everybody is sleeping, nobody knows that there was a miracle and the problems are all solved. (*pause*) So, when you are slowly waking up, what would be the first small sign that will make you wonder whether there was a miracle during the night and all the problems are solved? How would you discover this?

This is a carefully modulated, very long question designed to help clients use their imagination to see a picture of a solution. Even so, many clients respond with, "I don't know . . ." When this happens, it is important for the coach to remain quiet and not interrupt the client's deep state of concentration on new thoughts. Clients will slowly come out of their concentration, beginning with deep breathing, and either sit back or stay intensely focused on their imagination. Their facial muscles relax and one can easily see that something has shifted in the client's state of mind.

Client: I suppose . . . I would be calmer, a kind of peace of mind . . . I would look forward to the day instead of dreading facing the day, and I would want to get up, instead of wanting to stay in bed.

Coach: So, suppose you feel this peace of mind, want to get up and face the day. What would be the first thing you would do that you didn't do this morning?

Client: I would be eager to get to work, walk into the building with confidence, and say good morning to everybody.

The next step is to map out the details of this special day in interactional terms, that is, what the client would do, what others would do, what would come next, what else would follow that is different, and so on. It will take some practice to become comfortable and skillful in using this powerful tool.

> **TIP FROM THE FIELD**
>
> A very simple question, when clients describe their goals in terms of what they do not want, is to simply ask them, "What do you want instead?"

Even though it is called the miracle question, the solutions it generates are very realistic and doable because the details of miracle are generated by the client who knows his or her real-life circumstances.

Susan and the Two Bosses, Part 1

When Susan called, she said her work situation had become almost unbearable following a reorganization of the company. She was appointed as an assistant to two bosses instead of one, and both were preoccupied with their own changes in their jobs. They absolutely ignored her efforts and only worried about increasing their power in the company. Her autonomy and ability to make independent decisions were taken away and it seemed like the two bosses were competing to see who could micromanage her more. What made things even worse was that at age 55, she felt that her chances of getting an equal or better position were close to zero in a tight job market, and she had no time to look for another job. It was clear that she did not want to begin at the bottom and work her way up all over again in some other company.

When asked about her goal for the first session, she said she had to find a way to tolerate her current situation better, which was impossible for her to even imagine. The second choice was to find an alternative job option, which she thought was highly unrealistic, given the job market and her age.

When asked the miracle question, her demeanor began to brighten and the following conversation took place.

Susan: Well, I guess I would wake up and look forward to the day, a working day. I would look into the mirror like a competent and appreciated woman who does a good job, and I would be aware of all my resources.

Coach: OK, and what else will be different tomorrow morning and the rest of the day?

Susan: I would be able to keep a healthy distance at work, and take better care of myself, and think about my well-being.

Coach: So suppose you do. What exactly would you do differently that you are not doing right now?

Susan: I will have more energy and power and I will probably call an old girlfriend and go out to eat, which I haven't done for months. I've turned down every invitation because I've been so exhausted.

Coach: So suppose you go out with your girlfriend. Knowing you very well, what will this girlfriend notice that will tell her that a miracle has happened to you?

The conversation eventually turned to her two bosses. She thought that she would behave more assertively with them.

Coach: Susan, suppose you become more assertive with both bosses. How would they recognize that you are becoming more assertive with them without you saying it to them?

Susan: I guess Robert might become a little more polite, maybe even say "hello" or "please" and "thank you" to me. Maybe he would even compliment me on some work I have done. That would be a huge miracle—then I would be sure he has noticed that he is dealing with a competent woman who deserves respect.

Coach: And suppose he said something nice about your work. How would you then react to him?

Susan: I would probably smile and say that I am pleased to hear that. When I am alone, I would think, "Bingo!" and decide to treat myself to a trip to the spa that evening.

Just having a map of where we want to go is the first step of a thousand-mile journey. Since the next step of carrying out the plan depends on the client, and not on

TOOLBOX
Find out about goals. In real life: What does the client want to achieve in the real-life environment? Within the session: In consequence, what needs to happen in the session today?

the coach, the next phase of discussion must center on what the client needs to do to carry out which step first, and what comes second, third, and so on.

SCALING QUESTIONS

We could easily become excited about Susan's wonderful view of a miracle for herself, including a well-deserved and relaxing evening at a spa, being pampered and well taken care of. However, before we forge ahead, it is helpful to ground the vision of success to her reality, because she cannot force her bosses to behave as she wishes them to. This is where the use of scaling questions can be very helpful in turning a special miracle into reality. Listen to the following conversation between Susan and her coach:

Coach: After listening to what you have just said, I am going to ask you another strange question. On a scale of 1 to 10, 1 stands for the moment when you decided that the situation at work must change, that it cannot go on, and 10 stands for the morning after the miracle. Where on this scale are you right now?

Susan: I would say I am at a 3.

Coach: Wonderful. So what helped you to go all the way up to 3?

Susan: Just knowing that I can say to myself that I deserve respect from my boss and knowing that I am a competent person helped me move up to 3.

Coach: And the examples you talked about—the dinner out with a girl-friend, a compliment from Robert, the evening at a spa. Suppose you actually carry them out. What number would you say they would put you at on the same 1 to 10 scale?

Susan: Dinner out is a 6; the spa is a 7 because I made up my mind to do it myself, and getting Robert to appreciate me would be a 9.

Coach: Now I am going to ask you about a different 1 to 10 scale this time. Ten means that you have every confidence that these other things will happen, and 1 means you have no confidence at all that these things will happen. What number would you say you are at right now?

Susan: I would say my overall confidence is at 5 or 6. As I said, I can do the dinner and spa anytime I decide to do it. Getting Robert to com-pliment me on my work—I am not so sure, and that's where I am a little bit cautious.

Coach: That's amazing, 5 or 6 on your confidence.

Notice how the coach highlighted Susan's scale of 5 or 6, instead of her lack of confidence on ways to influence her boss. The choice of topic and area to emphasize is the coach's job, and it makes a huge difference. Suppose the coach emphasized her lack of confidence about influencing her boss. The conversation would certainly have taken a downward turn. Of course, she has no way to make her bosses behave a certain way, but there are many things she can do to make herself feel better, such as going out socially with girlfriends, going to a spa, and so on.

Any information a coach wants to know and any information that will further support a client's progress can be put in terms of a scale. It is not a hard and fast measure of objective data, but a subjective reflection of how clients perceive their lives. Therefore, we strongly suggest that you become comfortable experimenting with scaling questions. Scales can easily replace words, because there are times words are quite inadequate to measure personal experience.

The scale indicates changes that clients make so that they can see how far they have come and how far they have to go yet to reach their goal. One warning: It is important to give parameters of what 1 and 10 stand for so that clients can assess their own situation and evaluate what they need to do. However, there is a tendency in our culture to think that 10 means that life is perfect.

> **HOT QUOTATION**
> "If you want to be fast, go slow."
> —*Lao-tzu*

We do not assume that anybody's life is ever perfect. Therefore, it is more helpful to phrase the question in realistic terms by saying, "One means how upset you felt when you decided to call me to set up the appointment and 10 stands for 'I feel like I can go on with my life on my own without further help.' Where would you say things are right now?" We list some examples of how to phrase scaling questions. You can expand their use as much as your creativity will allow. Feel free to experiment with different uses and find what fits you and your clients.

- On a scale of 1 to 10, 1 stands for having no confidence at all and 10 stands for all the confidence you will need to make your decision to be assertive at work. What number would you say you are at right now between 1 and 10?
- What tells you that you are at 6?
- How long would you say you have been at 6?
- What is different with you now that you are at 6?
- What would your best friend see that tells him or her that you are at 6?
- Suppose you move up to 7. What would you do then that you are not doing right now?
- On a scale of 1 to 10, where 10 stands for the most proud you have been of yourself, how close would you say you are to 10 right now?
- How badly do you want to work to become the kind of person you want to be? Let's say that 10 means you will do just about anything you need to do to achieve it and 1 means you are just going to do nothing and wait to see what happens. What number would you say you are at right now?
- How hopeful are you that you will be able to complete your task? This time, 10 means that you are very hopeful and 1 means you are not hopeful at all?
- How come it is not minus 2?
- What are you doing to keep it from sliding down further to minus 5?

- What do you know about yourself that tells you that you would be able to reach 10 someday?

Exceptions That Light the Path to Solutions

The idea of exceptions was one of the first that the team in Milwaukee discovered in late 1970s that led them to formulate the solution-focused approach.[*] Exceptions are times when problems could have happened but somehow they did not. All problems have exceptions. Therefore, instead of paying attention to when, why, where, who, and how problems occur, when we begin to pay attention to how exceptions occur (with all the details of what, who, where, why, and when) the changes seem to occur much more rapidly.

Therefore, whenever we listen to clients' descriptions of problems that compelled them to seek coaching, we can at the same time ask about the times when the problem is a little less severe. Therefore, for example, find out about when the client is more at peace, feels calmer and more confident, more open and able to reach out to people. This will give client hope that they can repeat the successful strategies so that peace of mind will be likely

---

[*] de Shazer, S., Berg, I. K., Lipchick, E., Nunnally, E., Molnar, A. Gingerich, W., Weiner-Davis, M. (1986). Brief therapy: Focused solution development. *Family Proscess, 25,* 207–221.

to return through their control, rather than seemingly appearing out of thin air.

Hidden miracles, thus, shrink the size of obstacles that get in the way because they become less overwhelming, which in turn restores confidence that clients can decrease the frequency of problems. Existing glimpses of the miracles also show what needs to be repeated, thus lighting the path toward a more satisfying life for clients. For example, Martin sought coaching because he did not know how to get his reports written on time. He said that he sweated buckets every time he had to write reports. Because of the ever-changing business climate and constantly changing banking rules, he felt immobilized and did not know how to finish the reports that his boss asked for.

The coach recognized that Martin had finished college and must have written some papers to complete his college education, so she asked about it. Martin replied that yes, of course, he had written many good papers and he did not have a problem with finishing academic papers. The coach

> **QUESTION FROM THE FIELD**
>
> "What if I do not feel comfortable working with the client's goal?"
>
> It is our understanding that clients usually have good reasons for defining their goals, so maybe it can be useful to find out more about those good reasons first. If you feel you are not the client's best resource for working with a specific goal, say so and help your client find another coach.

asked for more details about how he managed to finish such boring papers. Martin did not realize, until he was asked, that indeed he did write many papers and got passing grades, and he did graduate from college. Then the coach asked, "What's the difference between writing college papers and writing reports on banking?"

Martin remembered that he did not take his studies seriously during his college days because he was care-free and single, without the responsibility of a wife and a child that he currently had. The coach asked whether he did better when he did not take his job too seriously. Perhaps so, Martin thought. It was difficult for the coach to suggest that the client slack off on his job. The coach finally asked how long Martin had his current job. About 2 years, Martin replied. The coach asked how many reports he had produced since he got this job at the bank. This is a good example of how a client can forget about previous successes in completing similar tasks. When the coach makes the connection between previous success and current tasks, the client can remember past successes and repeat them with more confidence.

USEFUL LANGUAGE SKILLS

Since conversation is more art than science, we can only become better at using language as our primary tool by becoming fluent in many possible ways to use this important tool. Along with the useful questions listed in previous sections, we want to describe few more useful attitudes and postures that point toward what to say and how to say it elegantly and simply, while building close collaboration with clients.

Plainly Speaking, Throw Away Jargons

Many coaches forget at times that certain words act as shorthand for communication among professionals. When they forget this fact, they tend to use professional jargon with clients. Have you ever heard medical professionals in hospitals—doctors, nurses, laboratory technicians, physical therapists, and so on—talk to patients as if they are talking to each other? They use medical jargon and technical words when they talk to patients and their families. Many patients are too intimidated to ask questions and professionals lack the time to explain things in plain language. A similar thing can happen with coaches. We strongly believe that use of jargon creates distance between coaches and their clients. For example, we often hear coaches saying to their clients, "I hear you saying that you get upset when someone does not hear you." Whenever you are automatically thinking about talking to clients this way, ask yourself "Would a gardener say that?" For example, how many people at work say to someone, "I hear you saying . . ." When we hear someone talk this way, immediately we might be tempted to say, "Don't talk like I am your client, please!"

We have a colleague who insists that we should use 5 dollar words, instead of 5,000 dollar words. I once heard a policeman ask, "Who resides in your domicile? Instead of saying, "Who lives with you?" Using common, everyday language tells clients that they can speak to us and we can understand each other.

The Power of Silence

Most people misunderstand and misuse the power of silence in conversation. Many assume that when clients are silent, it means nothing is going on in their brains and that they are either indifferent, unwilling to cooperate, or nothing is going on to contribute to the conversation. We think otherwise. Actually, we have come to appreciate the power of silence a great deal. The length of silence that is tolerable seems to depend very much on culture. For example, Native American clients generally tolerate long periods of silence, which they call thinking time, of up to 10 or 15 seconds, while the average American can find 5 seconds of silence painful to tolerate. When a coach can tolerate 5 seconds of silence, then he or she can be comfortable with what seems like an interminable silence to most clients. It is a matter of training in being comfortable and allowing clients ample room to consider the unusual questions used in brief coaching.

For example, when clients are presented with scaling questions or a miracle question, they can take a long time to respond because it can be startling to be asked to translate such intensely emotional experiences into measurable and countable numbers. But the outcome can be very enlightening for clients, because it forces them to become more thoughtful in an objective, measurable manner, which is very much needed in dealing with tough situations they are facing. For many intense situations and emotions, words may fail to convey one's experiences. Again, scaling questions can be very useful.

> **HOT QUOTATION**
>
> "You cannot solve a problem with the same kind of thinking that lead to the problem"
>
> —*Albert Einstein*

The Elegant Instead

Clients frequently present their outcome of coaching as an absence of problems, rather than a presence of solutions. For example, we commonly hear statements such as these:

- I want to stop being so bossy with my staff.
- I won't be grumpy with my staff in the morning, even though I am not a morning person.

- I won't procrastinate about everything. It takes lots of energy just to decide when to get the paperwork done, so I just keep putting it off.
- It is exhausting to decide whether I want to speak up at a meeting or not. Then I kick myself all day afterward.

These are some examples of how clients often begin sessions, by stating what it is that they want to eliminate from their daily life. Yet it is difficult to measure or notice the absence of something. After all, when clients notice progress, they became much more encouraged and it helps them to be more motivated to repeat the success. This is where the simple word *instead* enters to help the coach and the client to be clear about what it is that the client is looking for:

- So, what would you do instead of being bossy?
- Good idea not to be grumpy in the morning. How do you want to be instead?
- Yes, of course, it wastes a lot of your time. So what would you do instead?
- Suppose you do not hesitate at meetings. What would you do instead?

It is simple, but it takes discipline to get in the habit of listening to clients' words and then recognizing that they need some small help in defining desirable behavior, so that they can experience the reward of changes immediately. Of course, it encourages more changes.

Joining Both/And

Do you ever pay attention to how we use language every day? We are ultimately limited by the language we speak, although we also shape the language we speak. Thus, when language limits our thinking and ability to express ourselves, particularly in the field of coaching which primarily uses language as its tools, it is important that we professionals become sensitive to its limits as well as advantages. Most languages force us to think in dichotomies, that is, in either/or and black/white terms. Such limitations can create artificial limits on our creativity and how we think about things. Yet human beings do not come in simple black-and-white categories. Language also needs to reflect this reality. Therefore, we want to emphasize a wonderful method of joining many sides of our complex minds and thinking by using the concept of both/and.

Whenever you are tempted to say *but* to what the client said, the implication is that you disagree with what the client said. The word *but* tends to dispute or discount what the client said, thus making him or her feel put down, set aside, and disregarded. It is not a positive thing to do when your task is to encourage someone to consider alternatives to what is not working.

On the other hand, *and* implies that you accept what the client did or said, and you are just adding to what is there already. The message is that by adding to what was already suggested or accomplished you can move forward together. This is a wonderful way to collaborate with clients. Here are some examples of *and* questions:

- That must be a terrible thing to have happened—I can image. And what do you want to see happen instead?
- I see that you really tried many things already, and which one would you say worked the best for you so far?
- Of course, you have very good reasons to be upset, and what needs to happen here today that would be helpful, even a little bit?
- I can see what makes you think that your boss is out to get you, and what do you think he might say that he wants you to do instead?

How Instead of Why

Most people want to know the reason behind "dumb" things that people do and naturally want to get at what made the client think in an "incorrect" manner. The thinking behind this search for the cause is to make sure that such mistakes or wrongheaded thinking can be elim-

> **CASE FROM THE FIELD**
>
> What to do when the miracle is a disaster. At times, the client's answer to the miracle question is quite the opposite of what we think will make life better. For example, a client's answer to the miracle question was, "My husband will drop dead." When this happened to Insoo, without missing a beat she asked the woman, "Suppose he did drop dead, which certainly is unlikely. What would you do then that you are not doing right now?" The woman paused for a long time and said, "I suppose the first thing I would do is visit my daughter in California." She and Insoo were on the way to creating an alternative future for the client. Later the woman actually went to California, although the husband was still alive, of course. Not being stopped by barriers but getting around them can open up creative alternative routes to solutions.

inated so that the problem will never occur again. A noble cause, indeed. However, when we try to solve problems, asking *why* questions implies that somebody made a mistake and a finger is pointed at the person who is asked the question. Rather than helping us get at the desired change, this helps to make the person defensive and reluctant to confess to a mistake. This can easily lead to an argument, sulking, or defensive moves such as attacking the one who is criticizing. One can easily imagine an argument breaking out any second.

What should we do instead? A *how* question is a wonderful substitute and *how come* is even better because it encourages clients to explain what they were thinking when they did something unproductive or negative. When used with the right tone and inflection, *how come* questions soften the blaming, accusatory flavor that *why* questions can convey. Listen and compare the following questions:

Why are you late this morning?	How come you are late?
Why do you always do it that way?	How come you do it that way?
Why is it so difficult for you to do it right?	How come it is difficult? Please explain so I can better understand.

Of course, the proper use of intonation, facial expression, and gestures makes a world of difference.

"Suppose . . ."

Throughout this book, you will see many examples of how to make use of *suppose*—a wonderfully small word that does a huge job of helping clients use their own imagination to create solutions, as if pulling a rabbit out of a magic hat. This simple but powerful word makes it possible for clients and coaches to skip over the problem and get to details of the solutions and desired changes in the future. Whenever you feel like you need to pull an answer out of a magic hat, remember to use this small word to get a head start on possible solutions.

One can easily imagine many creative solutions not only through the eyes of the client but also through the eyes of others such as children, bosses, colleagues at work, best friends, and even pets. For example, a young man who owned three dogs talked about the dogs as if they were his children, describing each dog's unique personality and how each one came to live with him. When it was time to talk about miracles, the coach asked, "Suppose I ask your dogs how they could tell that a miracle has happened to you without your telling them about it. Supposing they could talk, do you have any idea what your dogs might say? How could they tell that there was a miracle for you and this is your brand new special day?" The young man had no difficulty with this question. As if it was the most natural thing, he immediately said, "My dogs could tell because they would notice that I am more attentive to them and more playful with them in the morning. They love that, you know. I guess I have been neglectful of them lately. I'm sure they miss my old self. I was more fun and we would wrestle on the floor."

"Good Reasons"

The two words *good reasons*, when used in a curious, inquisitive tone of voice, can do wonders when you want to find solutions to nagging, irritating problems. For example, Gary was sent to see a coach by his employer, who was really concerned about his health, lack of exercise, and tendency to work too many hours without a break. When the coach began negotiating the outcome of the session, Gary reported that his boss insisted that Gary become "less reliable and care less about my job," and "reduce my preoccupation with my work and become less responsible" through coaching. The coach was a bit shocked by this request from his boss, who was paying for the service, to help Gary become more lazy. The coach leaned forward and said to Gary, "I am sure your boss has a good reason to insist that you become less reliable and responsible." "Oh, yes, he does," he said and then explained that he had been working so hard, with no vacation and no exercise, eating fast food at his desk, and working long hours, that his wife was threatening a divorce and his doctor was warning him about a potential heart attack or stroke. Of course, his boss had good reason to be worried about Gary.

Tentative Language

Often called collaborative language or the language of negotiation, tentative language is a wonderful conversation strategy that all coaches should know. Here are some examples:

- I wonder about how realistic it is to . . . ?
- Perhaps so. . . . On the other hand, it seems like you might pay a pretty high price. What do you think?
- It seems like it could happen, I suppose . . .
- It appears it would only take a very simple tool, and it looks like an easy task. However, do you know someone who has successfully accomplished this? Have you ever seen it done?
- Could it be that you are thinking . . .

The advantage of this tentative language is that it allows you to disagree without alienating or offending the other person. If you say, "Oh, I am not sure about that . . ." it softens your disagreement with the client when you might want to challenge the client's view or statement. Since we believe that the client's future is created and negotiated, becoming fluent in these conversational strategies is very helpful and effective. We always prefer to influence the client to make good decision.

> **TIP FROM THE FIELD**
> Ask for hidden miracles. "When has there been a time recently when small pieces of the miracle have already happened?"
>
> Note that the question starts with when and not has, thus presupposing that there are always hidden miracles to be discovered. Also note that asking for small pieces helps clients come up with an answer.

Most of the time, not confronting the client with a direct attack or criticism leaves room to negotiate a more workable outcome.

It has been said that willingness and ability to use these low-key, nonconfrontational, nonoffensive language tools comes when a coach has a high level of comfort with his or her ability to put the client's needs first, without the need to have the client validate how smart or bright the coach is.

"What Else?"

You might at times ask the client a simple question: "What do you suppose your colleagues would say you do to contribute to the team?" The client may answer right away. Experiment with waiting for a few seconds after the client's first answer, then ask, "What else would they say you do to contribute to the team?" The client will give more details. The coach should accept this appreciatedly. Then the coach can ask again, "What else?" Wait a few seconds for the client to respond with more information. One can ask "What else?" up to five times on the same topic.

The beauty of this question is that clients will give details of compliments from others, or their successful management of difficult situations. The longer the list of accomplishments, the more clients come to realize that they indeed have made much more progress than they thought. In other words, asking the simple question "What else?" allows clients to compliment themselves. What better way for the coach to be lazy?

ADDITIONAL TASKS OF THE FIRST SESSION

Now that we have listed the useful tools of the coaching conversation, it is time to add a few more tasks of the first session. We view the first session as very important, not only because it sets the tone for the ongoing coaching relationship but because in about half to two-thirds of cases, it may be the only time you meet the client face to face. Therefore, it makes sense to make the most of the first session to create the most impact.

It is our task to accommodate the client's needs and negotiate realistic and achievable outcome goals. As you have seen, during this phase of contact we ask many unusual questions that perhaps clients have not heard before. Good questions generate new and helpful answers. Obviously clients may have asked similar questions of themselves, but having to say the answers out loud creates an entirely different effect on clients because they are forced to formulate the ideas in a much more concrete manner. If clients knew to ask themselves the same kind of questions that we ask during the first session, they most likely would solve their problems on their own. And many of them do.

Thinking Break and Feedback

It is a good idea to give yourself and clients a short thinking break that can be used as a transition from problems to solutions. A thinking break signals to clients that you are taking their words and concerns very seriously. You have collected enough information to get an early assessment of the client's situation, and you are thinking about next steps. After listening to and observing clients intensely, a coach begins to form an idea of what has worked and what has not.

While you take a brief thinking break, it is a good idea to put some physical distance between you and the client. You may want to ask the client to return to the waiting area or go out to get some fresh air. For the coach, this phys-

---

READER'S EXPERIMENT

Keep a diary of respected resources. Peter sometimes surprises coaching practitioners in workshops with a little present. It looks like any normal diary and on the tag it says "diary of respected resources." He explains that he has spent years in research with the Swiss paper industry to create a special paper that will only accept and make visible writing about things that you did well in your coaching sessions, observations about your growing resources as coach, and small hidden miracles even within sessions that did not go so well. You can experiment, taking notes after your coaching sessions, pretending that you are writing on this very special paper, and taking into account only things that you want to continue doing.

ical distance from an intense emotional and intellectual interaction gives a fresh perspective on the client. The thinking break is particularly useful if you sense tension between you and the client, or if you are unclear about the next step. We need clarity and an objective view of the client's goals and potential paths to achieve them.

Feedback to clients is our way of acknowledging that we have listened carefully to what concerns them the most, along with their list of successes, and indicates whether the goal seems worthwhile. Feedback indicates the general direction of where energy should be focused next and might offer some ideas for how the client could experiment in a real-life environment. This ending can summarize what has been learned, what has been tried, what to leave behind that is not working, what remains to be taken care of, and some negotiation of the next step. Whether to meet again, when, and how—whether in person, on the phone, or through e-mails—and how these contacts will be paid for can be discussed during the rest of the session.

Feedback has three components: compliments, a bridging statement, and suggestions for what might follow, what to pay attention to, or steps that will help the client move forward. This can be explained at the beginning of the session:

Coach: Before I begin, I would like to explain what you can expect to happen today. I am going to learn much about you and your hopes for this coaching. We will talk for about 40 to 45 minutes and then I am going to ask you to go out to the waiting area again for about 5 minutes. During this time I will sort out all the things you are about to tell me about what you want changed. I will need about 5 minutes to think about what you said, and then I will come back and share my thoughts with you.

You may notice that clients become very curious about your coming feedback. They are usually attentive and listen carefully.

Compliments

Begin with compliments, listing all the success stories you heard during the session. For instance, Susan was very realistic about her job situation and was acutely aware of what was possible and what was not. The coach might mention that it is good to be cautious and deliberate about such important decisions as whether to change jobs. Also, her idea of not wanting to start at the bottom of the pile makes sense. She had many creative ideas of how to take care of herself, such as seeing friends more, treating herself to a spa, and looking for practical solutions such as exploring ways to keep the current job more tolerable instead of jumping out of a bad situation.

It is common to observe clients nodding their heads and adding more validating comments. Some clients even break into tears of relief to hear that they are on the right track, that they are not messing up their lives, and, if anything, they are doing much better than they had feared. Many sit back, relax, breathe a deep sigh, and finally appreciate that they have done many good things and have been moving in the right direction.

For example, a manager of a small and steadily growing service company with 70 employees, who thought he faced a huge communication problem, listened attentively to the coach's feedback at the end of the first session and said:

Client: I am glad to know now that I am on the right track, and I have been doing the right things. I thought I had to figure out how to communicate with a growing number of employees. Well, I am happy to know that I am moving in the right direction and I just need to keep doing it. What I really wanted to find out was what I am doing is OK and I can continue to do what I have been doing. I think I can do that much easier.

Bridging Statement and Suggestions for Tasks

When a coach wants to support and encourage clients to keep doing what works for them, it is a good idea to comment on why it is a good idea. For example, during the interview the coach learned that the manager of this small company was already soliciting and listening to his employees' ideas and opinions on how to manage increasingly complex communications needs with an increasing number of employees. Therefore, the bridging statement was designed to explain to the manager why it was a good strategy to keep doing what he was already doing. The next step was a suggestion to watch out for other indicators that his strategies were continuing to work. The following bridging statement and the task flow naturally from the compliments and suggestions for what to do more of.

Coach: George, the more I listen to you, the more I am impressed with your basic understanding of what a good manager needs to remember: Every worker wants to be heard and respected for their ideas to improve productivity and contribute to the company. As we discussed, since you already know how to be a good manager, and you are already moving on the right track, the next step is to keep doing more of what you have been doing, because it is working. The only suggestion I can offer you at this point is to pay attention to what else you notice that tells you that what you are doing works for you and your company.

This kind of feedback is offered to clients at the end of the session in a majority of cases. However, sometimes we may need to suggest that clients do something different because what they are doing may not be working for them.

Do Something Different

Situations where we may need to suggest to clients that they should be doing something different occur in a small minority of coaching sessions, primarily because we are very good at detecting what clients do that works, even for a short time, and our task is to encourage clients to keep repeating what works until they are satisfied with their progress. This approach also leads to a brief coaching. Learning a new behavior takes time and repetition, which takes a great deal of effort, even with good motivation. But doing more of what the client knows how to do already is quicker and simpler, although it certainly is not easy because we tend to forget to do what works.

In some cases, however, it becomes very clear that the client needs to do something very differently because whatever he or she is doing is not working. Perhaps we can illustrate this type of situation best with an example.

QUESTION FROM THE FIELD

"Do you have to hold compliments until the end of the session?"

Of course we use all opportunities during the session to compliment clients. Whenever we are impressed with what clients tell us, we might also use some indirect complimenting:

Exclamations of appreciation *wow, amazing, really?*

Affirming the difficulty of the task: "I bet that was not an easy thing to do!"

Curiously asking to learn more: "Tell me, how did you manage to do that?"

Our colleague Ben Furman came up with the name "the triple" for this particular form of inviting clients to talk about solutions.

The New Supervisor

Margaret became a manager in a health care service system when the former manager retired without much notice, taking advantage of a new offer of an attractive retirement package. Margaret applied for the position and quickly got the job. Then she found herself in an awkward position of managing her former peers suddenly without any training. It frequently occurs that top-quality workers become managers overnight when there is an abrupt personnel change.

To prove to top administration that promoting her was a wise choice, Margaret was very eager to do a good job. She also desired to show her colleagues that their relationship had changed drastically. One of her duties as a supervisor was to countersign all outgoing mail to make sure that external relationships were managed according to company policy. Within two days of becoming a supervisor, she began to make liberal use of her red pen to make corrections on spelling and wording according to company policy. She was so eager to impress external contractors as well as her staff that she crossed out grammatical mistakes in red ink and sent documents back to her former peers to redo and submit to her again, with instructions attached.

Her former colleagues were irate and shocked at this procedure—which their retired supervisor had ignored. A few of her former colleagues who also applied for the same promotion were even more irate. Word spread like wildfire and the staff began whispering about her management style. Her former colleagues stopped talking to her and avoided eye contact when they passed each other in the hallway. Margaret decided to seek coaching soon after this episode because she could not tolerate the situation any longer.

Margaret was so shaken up by this situation that she did not know what to do. She was practically in tears recalling her humiliation and embarrassment in front of her former peers. She ruled out her first impulse to quit the job and get another job with a different company because she decided that she wanted to change jobs based on her strengths and not on her failure. The coach was impressed with this decision and agreed to work with Margaret. The first thing they agreed on was not only damage control but a new beginning. Margaret needed to do something entirely different, which required new thinking. The following is a segment of the conversation that took place.

Coach: It sounds like clearly you need to do something entirely different.
Margaret: Yes, I agree! But what do I do now? I have been so shaken up that I am not sure if I am thinking clearly right now.
Coach: I am not sure yet. So let me ask you. How many supervisors would you say you have had in your career so far?
Margaret: I have had many, if we count those I had as a student.
Coach: Do you remember what your former managers might have done in a situation similar to this? The best ones, I mean.

Margaret: I had one lady supervisor that I liked and respected very much. That was many years ago, but I never forgot her. When she became a supervisor, she called the entire staff to a meeting on the first day. She brought some special food and coffee bought with her own money and she began telling us about her background, about her family, her professional experience. Then she mapped out her vision for the unit and she asked for everybody's help in getting there. What I really liked about it was that she laid out a vision that would lead to better patient care. When she asked all of us who would like to work with her, of course, everybody had to say yes.

Coach: You have a very classy lady as a role model. Is this the kind of manager you want to be?

Margaret: Yes, I have to tell you that I completely forgot about this lady.

Coach: Your situation is somewhat different, because your supervisor laid out her vision on the first day. But you are known to your team. So you will need to do something different from what this lady did. What is it that you would like your staff to know about you and what is your vision for the team? What kind of help do you need from them to reach your vision?

Margaret: I have been so upset that I have not even thought about what I need to do to repair the damage.

Coach: What do you think your team would like to hear from you, since they know you from having worked with you for quite a while?

Margaret: I think they could easily misunderstand me and think that I am throwing my power around and showing off to the team that I am the boss now.

Coach: OK, so what is it that you want them to know about you as a supervisor?

Margaret: I want them to know that I am not any different from them. We were equals for a long time. I guess they would want to know what kind of supervisor I will be and what they can expect from me.

Coach: You have a very good sense about what they want from you, I'm sure. So, suppose you call a team meeting. How would you invite them to this team meeting?

Margaret: I guess I will have to start over very differently. I am really ashamed and embarrassed about my stupid beginning.

Coach: I wonder if your team might want to hear this.

Margaret: Do you think? Would I want to hear this from me if I were them? I wonder what they want to hear from me and see me do.

Coach: I can see that you are beginning to ask some very good questions. I think we need to fill in the details of how you would like the meeting to go.

> **HOT QUOTATION**
>
> "If it works do more of it; if what you do does not work, do something different."
>
> —*Steve de Shazer*

Margaret: I think I would want my supervisor to be very honest and straightforward and open. I need to show them I am a human and make mistakes and I can learn from mistakes. I want to apologize to them and then lay out my vision for the department and ask for their help.

Even in the middle of a difficult situation, it is possible to engage the client's expertise on former colleagues, in this case relying on past experience of a very competent supervisor's way of setting the tone as a leader of the department with a vision. As you can see, the more detailed the picture of how the meeting will go, the better ideas the client will generate. This is truly doing something different. We believe that people everywhere are generous and are willing to give others a chance to correct their mistakes.

CHAPTER THREE

TASKS BETWEEN SESSIONS
AND FOLLOW-UP

Since we believe that most of the real work of making changes occurs in the context of the client's daily life outside of coaching sessions, it is quite common to make suggestions for an experiment to try between conversations. It seems to result in not only brief contacts but also lasting results. In this chapter, we take a close look at how to accomplish both effectively.

GUIDELINES FOR EXPERIMENTS AND TASKS

We think the term homework is somewhat misleading. Most people think of homework as something children do for school, and we are reminded of how we hated doing homework as children. Teachers usually assign homework as a means to practice something new. It is designed to be repetitive to help children master the new material. Teachers may also assign homework as a means to make up for a skills deficit.

Therefore we began substituting the word experiment to avoid the images called up by homework for those clients who did not enjoy it. Calling it an experiment indicates that it is not a cure that coaches will prescribe to students but implies playfulness. The outcome of the experiment is unknown. One can easily think of a mad scientist's crazy experiments that we grew up seeing in movies. Yet at the same time we want to express our belief that "doing is knowing." In our view, clients "doing" solution behaviors offer a great deal of insight and wisdom about how solutions are created and maintained. Therefore, we place a great deal of emphasis on concrete behavioral changes.

> **TIP FROM THE FIELD**
> When designing experiments move from smaller to larger and from simpler to more complex tasks. All assignments should be successfully accomplishable by the client.

In addition, rather than helping clients talk about doing, we would much prefer that clients act out their solutions outside of the coaching office in their own usual environment.

The Purpose of the Experiment

So what is the purpose of suggesting an experiment between sessions? The following guidelines will help you in designing some experimental tasks.

Because we usually think of ways to increase client competency and ability at every opportunity, we encourage clients to change through doing more of what they know how to do. Therefore, any skills, behaviors, or thinking the client reports that he or she knows how to do and anything that will contribute to the client's life getting better should be repeated and encouraged. The list of what to suggest will emerge during your interview when you listen carefully to any presession changes reported. Do not suggest an experiment that the client does not know how to do. It will tend to discourage them from learning about their intuitive sense. The more clients trust their own intuitive sense, the more likely they will discover more resources within themselves.

Encourage clients to do what is good for them in their familiar and natural setting. The more clients do what is good for them, the more successful they feel and of course the more confident they will become. Therefore, it is always more helpful to make broad suggestions for an experiment, rather than a small, narrowly defined prescription.

We think these criteria for suggesting experiments speak volumes about our respectful attitude toward clients. We have trust and confidence that they will do what is good for themselves, as well as knowing what is good for themselves. As long as it improves their lives within legal and ethical boundaries, we will accept their way of doing things as appropriate.

So what are the common tasks that seem to promote client success at making life a bit better?

Types of Suggestions: Thinking, Observing, and Doing

Thinking differently can be the most important beginning step toward making changes. For example, a client's goal was to think first, and then talk later, because, as she said, "I usually talk first, and then it's too late because the damage is already done." During the first interview she found the miracle question very helpful, because it gave her an idea of what she might do differently. Thinking differently is a logical way to begin the change process, even though it is not the only way. She sought coaching to get through a job interview "without shooting my mouth off." The following conversation took place shortly after she had a job interview, during which she reported that she kept thinking about the miracle picture.

Coach: I am impressed. Most people would find the job interview so stressful that they would not be able to remember anything helpful. What did you do to keep your mind focused on the miracle picture?

Client: I guess I forced myself to keep thinking about how I did not have to think about how nervous I am. I just imagined myself being calm and how everything would turn out OK.

Coach: Yes, I can imagine that, but you know, I am particularly impressed with the stress of the job interview. It sounds like you kept your cool and stayed confident.

Client: I guess I did, didn't I?

Coach: It sure sounds like you did this time. What do you need to do so that you will keep thinking first and talking later?

Client: Oh, I think I can do it again because I was pretty nervous about the job interview, but other things will not be as stressful.

Coach: I am sure you are right. So what do you have to do next time in a similarly stressful situation?

Client: Just keep thinking about that miracle picture.

Coach: How confident are you that you can keep thinking about that miracle picture? On a scale of 1 to 10, what number would you say you are at?

Client: Oh, I would say between 5 and 8.

Coach: There's a big space between 5 and 8.

Client: Yes, I know. Sometimes I think I did pretty good and sometimes I think I should have answered something differently. That's why there is such a gap. But you know, that's pretty good for me. I used to be like 3 and 8.

Going Slow Gets You There Faster

Because the client could remember the steps she took to remember her miracle pictures, she was able to describe in detail how she achieved her goal of getting through an interview without making a mistake. Therefore, we

101

know now that (1) this is something she knows how to do, and (2) it would be helpful for her to do more.

The next suggestion we can offer the client is to keep doing what works. Because coaches want their clients to do well quickly and achieve more, many coaches could easily become ambitious for their client to achieve more and get there faster. But it is important to go slow and stay simple. It takes enormous discipline for the coach to stay the course, so that clients do not get pushed into doing too much too soon. Keep repeating the same successful steps. For example, to keep thinking about the miracle picture was all that was needed for this client.

The following message was given to the client after a short thinking break. It is an example of how the coach can give compliments on what clients report that they have done is related to the goal. Even though this client was inspired by the miracle question the coach asked during the previous session, it is a good idea to explain the reason for suggesting the task and the next step that the client needs to stay focused on.

> **HOT QUOTATION**
>
> "A journey of a thousand miles begins with a single step."
>
> —Chinese proverb

Coach: Well, I want to tell you how impressed I am that you have done something very difficult for most people, that is, to stay focused while in a tough situation like the job interview. Not only did you pay attention to the interview process, which is difficult enough, but you were able to pay attention to many complex things that were going on and you knew when to keep remembering the miracle picture.

You learned form this experience that when you focus your attention on the miracle picture, you can accomplish many things. It is amazing that because your focus was so strong, even your confidence has gone all the way up to 5 and 8.

Clearly, the next step is to recognize when to use your ability to focus and keep doing what you are doing, that is, to stay focused on the miracle picture, especially when you are under stress. Pay attention to what you do and how other people react to your ability to think about the miracle picture. Let me know what difference this makes.

This three-part message (compliment, bridging statement, and suggestion for next step) should flow in a logical manner so that the client can see the rationale for doing the task. In this message, two tasks of thinking and observing were combined. The client was invited to keep thinking about the miracle picture because the coach knew she found it very useful, she knew how to do it, and she could do it again when the situation was not as difficult, since she did it successfully during the stressful situation.

The task should be always expanding outward, rather than contracting to a narrower focus. Many people are familiar with business and management meetings that end by narrowing down the options, rather than opening up and expanding them to wider possibilities. The task should be designed to leave room for the client to spontaneously improvise a solution, rather than constricting the solutions to a coach's idea of what might work and what might not. We have been quite surprised numerous times by clients' creative and surprisingly innovative minds that come up with solutions that we could not possibly have thought of.

Observation Task

As we mentioned before, sometimes thinking leads to noticing something different, which can lead to doing something different. People do not always change in an orderly manner and the same person does things differently at different times. You have probably had the experience of finding yourself doing something different, realizing that you have changed your routine, and then recognizing what has happened without your conscious intention.

We have found that clients do the same. We suggest that they think about, or just observe and

> **QUESTION FROM THE FIELD**
>
> "I am working with managers a lot, and they seem to expect to narrow down their options at the end of a coaching session. Should I talk them out of it?"
>
> They should be the experts on how they can make life better. Narrowing options down may work for them. However, if walking out of the coaching session with a tight action plan does not prove to work, we might suggest trying something else.

pay attention to what goes well in their life that they do not want changed. It is much more reassuring for clients to discover that there are many things going well in their life already.

EXPERIMENTS THAT BREAK THE PATTERN

Even though it is less common that we suggest that the client do something entirely different, it is more fun for coaches and clients because it allows lots of room to be creative and freely use one's imagination. In addition, even a small change can make a big difference in clients' hope and excitement at having a new way to approach the same frustrating difficulties. Since we discuss techniques to do something different extensively in Chapter 4, we suggest that you read it now if you wish and then return to this chapter again. We list some easy-to-do suggestions that fall under this category with positive results. Using your own creativity, you may want to come up with something that your clients might find helpful to break the pattern of failed attempts.

Pretend a Miracle Happened

When clients have a very clear and detailed description of a miracle day when their goals for coaching will be successfully achieved, and they seem willing to take the necessary steps to implement the desired solutions, a very good task to suggest is to pretend that the miracle has happened. Since coach and client could spend up to 20 or 25 minutes during the session discussing the miracle, many details of the solution picture would emerge. With a client who is willing to do something to begin the change process, it is a wonderful suggestion. You can also add that clients should not announce what they are doing to the world, but keep it private. They should notice who is the first to notice the changes in the client and what exactly other people do in response.

It is a good idea to negotiate with clients on which day of the week, or how many times between this meeting and the next they would be able to do the experiment. Again, more is not always better, but a strategically planned implementation is more useful. It should be simple and easy for the client to increase the likelihood that the client will actually implement it. Make it a lively, interesting, and fun exercise for the client to increase motivation to carry out the experiment. As they say, when you know what you are looking for, you are likely to find it.

Pretend You Have Moved Up One Point

It is a variation on the same theme to pretend the client has moved up one point. The only difference is that the coaching session would need to include discussion of the details of different scales. Clients would need to determine whether they tend to think in terms of a progression from 1 to 10 or in an incremental approach. Again, it is helpful to carry out the task in the workplace or in relationship to others clients interact with so that there are observable indicators that the changes are noticed and supported by others.

TIP FROM THE FIELD
Good ways to start sentences about experiment tasks:

"I agree that it is time to do something."

"Because you have convinced me how serious you are about getting on track ..."

"Part of me thinks your situation calls; for action, while another part of me thinks you must review this more ..."

Flip a Coin

Flipping a coin is very useful for clients who feel that their solution will require control from outside themselves, rather than self-control, for example. If they feel they have no control over their unwanted behaviors, it is not productive to try to convince them to take charge of their lives.

The Procrastinator

A highly intelligent, well-educated business executive, Mr. Taylor, has been plagued by his tendency to procrastinate all his life. He thought that he could be more productive if he did not waste so much time putting things off and kept moving on with his tasks. He felt desperate to change this bad habit that had persisted throughout his life. He reported that he had tried "everything known to mankind." Even though he certainly has had productive days occasionally, he described himself as getting into a slump and taking "a long time" to become productive again. When asked about how he got himself back on track and became productive again, he could not describe exactly what he did. It seemed like a coin toss might be a perfect solution. However, for a high-powered, highly educated, and successful executive like Mr. Taylor, the coach was concerned that he might think that basing his decision making on the random turn of a coin might seem like a absurd idea. The coach asked Mr. Taylor whether he was willing to try something he might consider out of the ordinary and even silly. He said he was desperate, and his willingness to try anything "ethical and legal" the coach might suggest was 9 on a scale of 1 to 10.

The coach gave Mr. Taylor a foreign coin that was left over from travels overseas, along with the following instruction. Beginning as soon as he returned to work in the early afternoon, he was to set the coin in a prominent place in his office. When his usual internal debate began, or when he was tempted to put things off as usual, he was to take the coin and shake it in his hands, flip the coin on the back of one hand, and observe which side came up. If it was heads, he was to force himself to get to the task at hand immediately, regardless of how he felt about it. If it was tails, he was to postpone carrying out the task, again regardless of what he felt like doing. Since he was a busy man with numerous tasks throughout the day, he wondered how long he should wait until the next toss of the coin. The coach and Mr. Taylor negotiated that there should be a wait of at least 2 hours between coin flips. The 2 hours of waiting was Mr. Taylor's idea, because he estimated that this is how much time he wasted.

Mr. Taylor returned 2 weeks later and reported how much better his life was going and expressed satisfaction with the help. Of course the coach was curious about how Mr. Taylor carried out the experiment. He explained that on several occasions he really did not like it when the coin told him to postpone performing the task at hand, so he kept flipping the coin until heads came up. Of course, the coach and Mr. Taylor had a joyous laugh together. While reviewing this experiment, Mr. Taylor got an idea that he might try using the coin at home also. Since it worked for him in the way he improvised, we ended the coaching with two sessions.

The Internet Surfer

Why did it work? We have no idea why it worked for Mr. Taylor and many other clients. It even worked with one young woman, Michele, who saw herself as a compulsive Internet surfer at work. She reported that she read somewhere that it was an addiction and asked whether coaching could help with addiction. It created a serious time management problem for her because she was always behind in her work and her boss had caught her looking at her monitor and laughing. At other times he caught her in a trancelike state, inattentive to what was going in her worklife. She was also tired of sneaking around and being hypervigilant about who was watching her. She felt like her life was getting out of hand and she began to fear losing her job. The same procedure of tossing a coin was suggested and in two meetings her surfing problem was under control. It did not go away, but she decided to toss a coin every hour or so and cut her surfing time to 10 minutes, which she thought was a vast improvement.

We all tend to resent being told what to do. Even if it is our own voices scolding us, the urge to

> **READER'S EXPERIMENT**
>
> It is not always easy to put things you have read into action. First of all, one never knows if a really good opportunity to try out things will present itself or not on a given day. Here is our suggestion for a prediction experiment: During the next 5 days, take a look at your daily schedule before you start to work and make a prediction. If you think you will be surprised by a wonderful opportunity to try out something you have read, mark the page with an X. If you think no useful surprising opportunity will pop up during the day, mark your calendar with an O. Take another minute at the end of the day to see whether you predicted correctly.

rebel against rules is strong. Yet at the same time, it seems easier to "just listen to a dumb coin," as one client put it. At times, it is nice not to have to make a decision, and just do what something or someone else tells us to do. When we are given so many choices and options for everything, as one client explained, it "is a relief not to have to follow rigorous discipline and just become a slob."

Prediction Task

Prediction is another helpful task for clients who seem to feel that they need to know what is ahead tomorrow or next week, or feel some kind of comfort in knowing that they can predict the future. Another group of clients who can benefit from this task are those who seem to undervalue their ability and assume that they are doing much worse than they actually are doing. Since there is no way to reassure some people who are constantly underrating their own abilities, it is best to have them rate their own performance so that they can convince themselves, rather than being reassured by the coach or someone else. Prediction is most effective when used in combination with the scaling questions.

There are two ways to carry out this task. One is to use the coin to predict whether tomorrow will be a good day or a bad day. Using a coin allows only two outcomes, either good or bad. The second option is to make a chart (Figure 3.1). Some clients love charts and graphs and

Day	Prediction (made on Sunday)	Outcome (check on Monday)
Monday	5	6
Tuesday	6	7
Wednesday	7	6.5
Thursday	6	7

FIGURE 3.1. Chart of predictions and outcomes.

many people respond to visual cues. As with all suggestions, it is important to provide a rationale for doing this
experiment that closely reflects the client's understanding of the difficulty. You might say something like, "We
need to see how you are actually doing because we need
to establish a baseline for finding the solution that will
fit your situation," and then explain the procedure. The
purpose is to show how much skill clients already have
in making good choices, although they may not recognize this ability.

When the client returns with this chart, you can find
out the details about both the prediction and outcome.
For example, let's suppose that the coach used a prediction experiment with Mr. Taylor. The coach can ask Mr.
Taylor about the experiment:

1. When Mr. Taylor made a prediction of 5 for
    Monday, what did he know about Monday's

schedule that told him that he might be as successful as a 5 on Monday?

2. When Mr. Taylor reviewed the chart at the end
   of the day, what was different about the day that
   made him perform slightly better than his own
   prediction? What surprised him about the day
   that made him see himself
   at a 6? What did he do differently than he antici-
   pated?

3. When Mr. Taylor predicted
   that he would be at 6 for
   Tuesday, what did he do
   during the day that helped
   him surpass his own prediction and end up at 7?
   What would his colleagues
   or his employees say they
   noticed that was different
   about him on Tuesday?

> **INTERESTING FACTS**
>
> A study conducted at BFTC showed surprising results. During a half-year period, no experiment tasks were proposed to clients. The success rate with these cases stayed almost identical around 85%; however, the number of sessions per client increased from 2.9 to 4.2.

4. What did he learn about
   himself from his experi-
   ment? How would he incorporate what he
   learned from this experiment into his life?

5. What does he need to do to maintain the 7
   level? If his life continued at the same level,
   would he say it is going quite well?

In the next section, we discuss how to follow up on the second and later sessions until it is time to say good-bye.

WHEN IT IS BETTER

Following a brief time spent in small talk about the terrible weather or a wonderful performance of your favorite football team, the most frequent way that second, third, and later sessions begin is for the coach to say, "So, what has been better since we met last time?" Another nice way to start is to say, "What is different in your life since we met last time?" Notice how this question is phrased. Instead of saying "Is anything better?" or "Has anything changed?," "What kind of changes have you made?," the coach is asking something quite different. Phrasing the question that assumes that something is bound to be better or different and we are interested in learning what that is, no matter how small the changes are. We have learned over the years that some clients feel pressured by the word better. We are primarily interested in what kind of changes clients have made, whether things are better, the same, or even worse.

Even when the question is phrased this way, whether it is the second or the tenth session, a large majority of clients will say, "Yes, a little bit," or "You won't believe what I tell you," or "I knew you were going to ask me that, so I've been thinking about it on the way over here." Generally clients tend to respond in one of three possible ways. A surprisingly large number of clients report positive changes, as in the following case of Susan, whom we met in Chapter 2. In a smaller number of situations, clients say, "About the same" or "Nothing is different." We want to, first, discuss how the majority of clients respond, that is, that things are better.

Susan and the Two Bosses, Part 2

After polite small talk about the weather, the coach started with, "So, Susan, what has been better since we talked last, even a little bit?" Two weeks had passed since the first meeting. Much to the coach's surprise, it seemed rather easy for her to answer the question. The big improvement, she reported, was that she had become much more able to tolerate her work situation.

Actually, it had become so good that she could now even imagine herself staying on the job and putting up with her two bosses, Robert and John. She reported that it was as though a huge burden had been lifted from her shoulders, and she was enjoying having a real choice of staying with the same job or not. Both options were imaginable to her now.

Coach: Well, I am truly impressed and relieved to hear that, Susan. If I may, I would like to come back to this in a minute. But first, tell me, what else has been better during these 2 weeks?

METAPHOR OF THE FLOWER GARDEN

Asking "What has been better?" is like going out to the garden and checking on the flowers. There may be a lily that has lost a couple of leaves, which lie on the lawn now. There may be a favorite rose that some kids must have damaged. At first sight, the rest of the flowers may look pretty much the same as they looked before. If you want to see what has been growing, you need to look more closely. You need to check back with your memory to notice small differences, and you need to select differences that represent some sort of growth process—somewhat like shining a flashlight, in the dark, when you are looking for something very specific.

Eventually you may make out a carnation that seems to have opened up maybe just a tiny bit more than last time. You might even need a magnifying glass to make out tiny petals that have not only grown but also gotten more vivid in color. Having found one detail of progress, suddenly you may notice much more proof of growth everywhere in your garden.

Susan reported she had really fallen in love with her little notebook of self-care and she was so proud of some of the things she had written in it that she had even read some of it to one of her closest friends. This reminded her that another thing that was better was her much more active social life. She had gone out with friends at least once every week, sometimes even on weekday evenings.

Finally, she saw an ad for a job that looked interesting, and she had even used all her courage to call them and ask some questions about the job. She followed up by actually applying for the job and was now waiting

116

for the response. She even mentioned that she was under less pressure to look for another job right now, because things had improved so much at work, even under the same two bosses. She decided that she would take a good look at the new job if given a chance, but she would take her time. She reported that it felt so good to have the pressure off her shoulders and she could take time to look around. The coach and Susan discussed how much difference it makes when one is making a decision to leave compared to feeling pushed to leave.

The first few minutes of the session were spent in getting a broad overview of all the different areas of her life that had gotten better. Amplifying the momentum of this small but significant success and finding out what else is better for the client builds a further foundation for more successes. We find that the longer the coach stays with the success story, the more confident the client becomes, and one episode will remind them of another example. After the long list of answers to the question, "What is better?" your attention can be focused on details of what the client did to create success, as the following dialogue shows.

Coach: Of all the things have become better, which one are you most proud of?

Susan: Probably at work, how Robert and John treat me like I'm a valuable and competent person.

Coach: Oh, they do?

Susan: John even put a thank-you note on my desk, when I had finished this report for him after 5 o'clock. Robert is much more polite. He greets me in the morning. Once he even asked me how I was managing having two bosses. I made this proposal to have incoming work organized more effectively. He accepted and said nice things about how I was always trying to be efficient.

Coach: How did you manage to do that? I would imagine it was not an easy thing to do.

Susan: Actually, it was easy. He is just so much more respectful of me now.

Coach: I see, so he is more respectful. Is there anything you might have contributed that made it easier for him to be more respectful? Do you have any idea what it could have been?

Susan: I think I know. It started a couple weeks ago, after I talked to you, when he came dashing into my office. I had heard him coming and I remember I looked him right in the eyes when he came in, like I was saying, "Yes, what is it that brings you here, young man, without even knocking?" I did not even say anything. I just calmly waited for him to start and for the first time, he said, "Susan, please," to begin with. It was like he knew I would not let him mess with me anymore.

On the progress scale, Susan reported she was now at a 6. Her confidence that she would be able to keep her current 6 was at 8.5. The major question left was to decide if she should invest more energy in finding a different job or just enjoy her success and stay on this job for a while. She really was not sure yet, but she was enjoying her current state of 6 for now. It was clear to her that she wanted to wait for the response to her recent job application and see what choices opened up for her. The coach told her that it took a great deal of confidence to be able to take time and weigh her options. During the remaining time of the session, we looked at how Susan could maintain her current feeling, still new and unfamiliar, of being val-

> **TIP FROM THE FIELD**
>
> When working with clients on a longer-term basis (e.g., within management development programs), start your session by checking if the client has any specific issues that he or she wants to cover during the session, so you can make sure there is enough time for the client's agenda. Before looking at the issues at hand, make sure you take some time to ask what has been better. Sessions generally turn out more productive if you begin by looking at resources first and dealing with challenges afterward.

ued by her bosses. We also examined how she might handle the normal ups and downs of this changing process. She agreed that it was strange to be in a place where she had never been before.

After the thinking break, the coach gave Susan compliments and expressed his admiration for all the things she had accomplished between the first and second sessions: taking good care of herself, gaining respect as a competent person in the workplace, and making the decision to wait and see what options opened up for her. There were only three sessions in total with Susan before she decided that she no longer needed coaching, but she would certainly return for further sessions if she needed it.

Giving Credit to the Client

Even when things have improved vastly, many clients tend to give credit to others or to circumstances. Effective coaching means helping clients to claim their just credit and feel comfortable owning their actions that created such positive changes. Rather than giving a stern lecture or offering unsolicited teaching comments, it is always more respectful to offer clients an opportunity to self-compliment. The following questions can set the stage for this to happen:

- What do you suppose you did to help make that moment happen?
- Where did you learn to do that?
- How would you explain what happened?
- Suppose your best friend had seen you do it. What would she have noticed about you and what would she compliment you on?
- You remember numbers questions? I am going to ask you some numbers questions here. Let's say 1 stands for how badly you felt you needed to change the situation with your bosses and 10 means that you got what you wanted from talk-

ing to me. What number would you say you are at right now?

- How confident are you, on a scale of 1 to 10, where 10 means that you are very confident of staying the course as things are right now? What number would you say you are at right now?

- What would tell you that you may be on the way to moving up one point higher on the scale?

Track the Changes

Our experience is that the majority of clients return saying that life is better in some way.

It is important for the coach to track the changes, either upward or downward. As indicated elsewhere, the fact that the client has taken the initiative to see the coach itself is already a positive step. Therefore, the first coaching session already builds on the client's initial changes.

The next step is to gather the details related to improvements

- What did you do to make the improvement?

> **QUESTION FROM THE FIELD**
>
> "How do you deal with clients who give all the credit for things being better to others?"
>
> Try saying something like, "Yes, of course, others were helpful. If there was one small thing that you might have contributed, what could that possibly have been?"

- Where did this happen?
- When did this happen?
- Who was involved?
- How did it happen? How did you make it happen that way?
- What would your best friend say about how she could tell that your work is getting better for you, without you telling her so?
- What else is better?

Whether the improvement is big or small, the coach needs to celebrate the success immediately and find out what steps clients took to make the improvement.

- Scale the improvement.
- Scale the level of confidence that the client can repeat the progress.
- A suggested task is to keep doing what works.

WHEN CLIENTS SAY NOTHING IS DIFFERENT

At times, perhaps no more than 20% or 30% of the time, the client response can be "It's the same" or "Nothing is different," indicating that they have not noticed any kind of improvement. Remember that not noticing improvement is not the same as not making improvement. At times, it seems from the client's appearance that he or she is doing better, but if the client's view is that there is no improvement, then it must be so.

"Being the same" means nothing has become worse. Therefore, it is a good sign that the client is doing something positive because the situation has not become worse. You can ask about what the client has done to keep things the same. The ability to keep things at the same level can be viewed as the client's ability to prevent a slide

> **CASE FROM THE FIELD**
>
> One of our workshop participants was taken by surprise by a client who said, "Nothing has been better!" Not expecting this answer, he was speechless and did not know what to say or do. It took him a long time to come up with something useful. Not getting much of a reaction from the coach, the client in the meantime had given it some further thought and finally continued, "Well, except for maybe last week when ..."

backward, which is a very helpful skill. Again, we are always looking for existing resources, competence, and ability to foster improvements. Teaching clients something new is not the first choice but a last resort.

The old reliable scaling question is very useful to find out the client's current status. Other useful information can be gained from scaling questions, as the following examples show:

- Let me ask you this way. On a scale of 1 to 10, where 10 stands for where you would like to be by the time coaching is over and 1 is the worst possible situation you felt you were in when you decided to call for coaching sessions, where would you say you are right now?

123

- What tells you that you are at 4?
- What is different now that you are at 4, compared to when you were at 1?
- Suppose I ask your best friend and colleagues at work the same question. What would they say they think about where you are on the scale?
- How have you been able to maintain a 4?
- What would it take for you to move up one point higher on the same scale?
- Suppose you move up one point higher. What would your best friend and colleagues see you do then?

In the process of answering these questions, clients frequently come to realize that they are in fact doing much better than they thought. Scaling questions have a way of slowing down the conversation because as people think about how they might evaluate themselves on the scale, it takes time. Therefore, make sure to allow longer periods of silence and time to think.

Curiosity is a useful stance because the more curious we become, the more curious clients also become about their own abilities. It can be infectious. For example, when the coach is curious about the client's ability to sustain a 4, the client also becomes curious about her circumstances and begins to become more observant. Again, we want to remind you that this kind of subtle curiosity is expressed with tone of voice, inflection, facial expressions, and posture.

Coach: You mentioned that you are at 4 now. Is that right? (*leaning forward*)

Client: Yeah, it feels about right.

Coach: How long would you say you have been at 4?

Client: Oh, I would say about a week or so.

Coach: Wow, that's a long time.

Client: I guess so. For me it is.

Coach: Yes. What have you been doing to make it stable for about a week or so?

The coach's curiosity can be verbally and nonverbally expressed. For example, leaning forward, raising eyebrows, picking up a pen and writing down what the client reports, and using inflection and voice tone all contribute to convey to clients that we are amazed by their successes. The coach can interrupt the client in midsentence, with a surprised look, and ask, "You did what!?" and lean forward as if this is the most amazing news the coach has ever heard. With curiosity, the client can begin to construct a new meaning for "what is better," "nothing is better," or even "things are worse."

WHEN CLIENTS SAY THINGS ARE WORSE

In a small number of cases, clients report that things are worse for them. In the past, out of shock, we had a tendency to just sit and think about what the client said. We learned that some clients would review their answers for about 10 seconds (which is, by the way, a long time in normal social conversations) and then might say, "There were some days when things were a little bit less frantic." We learned that this is time for the coach to perk up and say, "Tell me when was a little less awful. Which day was a little bit less bad than other days?" This can generate very useful descriptions of some amazing things clients did to help themselves. Therefore, it is very useful to take advantage of clients' silence to help them reflect on their small but significant successes.

When some clients respond to the question, "What is better since we met last time?" with comments like, "Better? Are you kidding? It's been worse!," it is easy to become disappointed and feel as if you have failed. In a small percentage of cases—perhaps as little as 3% of the time—clients will report that things have slid backward, instead of moving forward. Even though we may not want to hear this, being respectful of their views demands that we listen carefully to learn what made things worse.

Making the Ordinary Extraordinary

One of our colleagues, Gale Miller, is fond of saying that brief coaches are people who make clients' ordinary events into extraordinary accomplishments. Being an ethnomethodologist, he should know such things, but what he means is that brief coaches construct extraordinary events out of small, normal, almost invisible events of daily routine. If you listen to clients' background information, indeed a success usually is something that takes extraordinary persistence and hard work.

One of the important reasons we emphasize and insist on learning about clients' details of success or problems is that between big events that may be bad or good, the details may include surprisingly spectacular moments that clients often overlook. Many clients, and even coaches, misunderstand the word success or accomplishments to mean outstanding, extraordinary, or unusually large successes. We believe that life is made up of many little accomplishments, day in and day out.

> **HOT QUOTATION**
>
> "There is no real understanding of what others really want to tell us. There are only more useful misunderstandings and less useful misunderstandings."
>
> —*Steve de Shazer*

Ask Coping Questions

Rather than feeling helpless, begin to use coping questions (see Chapter 5 for more details). Some examples:

- How have you managed to get through all the terrible things that happened to you?

- How do you cope with all that's going on in your life right now?
- What was most helpful in getting through what you just went through?
- What would your best friend say you are doing that helps you to cope as well as you are?
- On a scale of 1 to 10, where 10 is where you would like your life to be, what number would you say you are at right now?

Even in the midst of the worst circumstances, the fact that the client has made it to the session, or has the presence of mind to talk to a coach, is an indication that the client is able to cope well enough to maintain a small degree success and some kind of normal routine. When we look at these small successes as huge successes in the context of the client's life, we cannot help but admire the client's determination and resilience to go on with life and accomplish many more things.

WHEN CLIENTS DO NOT FOLLOW SUGGESTIONS

Clearly it is reasonable to ask what to do when clients fail to follow suggestions. Some coaches have had this kind of experience and may feel a bit of frustration with the client. Another possibility is that coaches need to feel secure in knowing how to respond in case clients say they did not do the task. When coaches believe that the homework task is the answer or solution to a client's concerns, or believe that following such suggestions will definitely improve the client's situation, it becomes even more urgent to know. As we mentioned earlier, we do not believe this is the case. Quite the contrary, we believe that clients are the experts on their lives and they know what might or might not work in their unique circumstances. Therefore, we assume that the client has good reasons for not doing that task, which may include the following:

> **QUESTION FROM THE FIELD**
>
> "I sometimes run into clients who report back that the initial problem does not seem to bother them any more. Is it OK when they just feel better about the issue without actually having made any progress in solving the initial problem?"
>
> We have also had such experiences and we have learned that in many instances there seems to be no connection whatsoever between the problem presented by the client and solutions that prove to work. There can be limitations in life that cannot be solved. Yet clients can learn to effectively cope with them and thus feel sufficiently better about them.

- Perhaps it did not make sense to the client.
- It did not fit the client's way of doing things.
- Perhaps the client found a better solution than what the coach suggested.

It is always a good idea not to check up on whether the client has done the homework at the beginning of the following session, as a teacher might do with students. After all, clients are not little children in school and we are not teachers evaluating students' performance. Begin the second, third, and later sessions by asking what is better or what is different as explained above. You do not need to check up on clients, but it is a good idea to find out what they did instead, if they apologetically volunteer the information that they did not follow the suggestion. We believe that what clients decide to do is likely to be a better solution for them than anything coaches could conjure up. We do not want to be wedded to our ideas of what is good for clients.

A coach can always say, "I am glad that you did not do it. If it did not seem to be the right thing to do, then obviously I must have overlooked something important when I suggested it to you. What have you done instead? It was more helpful, I'm sure."

WHEN CLIENTS REPORT SETBACKS

We realize that nobody's life is a steady upward climb all the time, so we learn to appreciate good days and notice how we can get through not-so-good days also. We can appreciate success more and savor it longer. Many coaches become disappointed and even alarmed because they feel as if they have failed when they hear clients report a setback. This kind of reaction is infectious, and clients learn to feel the same. Of course we want our clients to always be successful, but that is not the reality of life. So what do we do when we hear bad news? Stay calm. Try the five-step approach that we have developed.

The Five-Step Model

Since it is a normal process of change, maintain your curiosity as you follow these steps.

Step 1

First of all, a setback means that at one time there was success. Without at least some small success, we would not notice a setback, but only see a continuing funk. Therefore, immediately ask about the period before the setback, when things were more normal and the client was doing well, including the period before the client decided to seek coaching help. Ask about what was different, what clients did that worked for them, and do not allow yourself or your clients to dwell on current failures and disappointment too long. It is often surprising how long clients have maintained a steady course of doing well, yet they can forget that so quickly. Here are some examples of useful questions:

- How were things different for you before this happened?
- What were you doing differently then?

- How would your best friend describe you during
  those days?

Step 2

Ask about when clients caught themselves and kept
from sliding back further than they did. For example, if
a client says she felt nonproductive for a whole day last
week, ask about what she did to stop it from becoming
2 days. What exactly did she do to make the funk last
only 1 day and not allow it to spill over into 2 days?
What gave her the clue that she was sliding backward,
and what did she do first thing to prevent a further
slide? What helped her avoid doing things that she did
not want to do, such as brooding, complaining, and
blaming other people openly?

Step 3

Ask what clients did as soon as they found out that
they were going backward. What was the first thing they
did to get back on track? What helped? Who else helped?
How did they know that exactly the right thing to do?
What difference did it make?

- What internal or external clues told you that
  you were experiencing a set-back?
- What did you do to get back to your usual routine?

- What did you find most helpful in getting back to your old self?

Step 4

Ask what was different about the current setback compared to the most recent one the client had. Being different means something is changing. How is the client making those changes? What else is different about this relapse? How did the client create a change this time? What would other people say about how the client made this change?

Step 5

Ask what lessons clients have learned about themselves from setbacks. How will they use and implement new lessons?

It is helpful for the coach to remember that human beings have an amazing ability to evaluate themselves. We are indeed privileged to participate in and witness these capabilities and events.

WHEN TO SAY GOOD-BYE

Because the majority of coaching cases tend to be brief, we assume each session could very well be the client's last. We accept the fact that we are a poor judge of how many sessions a client will need. Therefore we do not

> **CASE FROM THE FIELD**
>
> Asked about what had been better at the beginning of the fourth session, one of our clients answered, "I was almost sure you were going to ask that question. So on the way here on my bike I already started to come up with answers." It turned out to be the last session with that client, who had obviously learned to come up with useful questions by himself, with no further need to see a coach.

decide how many sessions a particular concern will take. How many coaching sessions are required is up to the client. This certainly is not good for the coach's income, but it is the ethical way to practice. Once you are known as a coach who can get clients in and out of coaching successfully and efficiently, your referral base will increase as your reputation spreads.

Scaling Questions to Monitor Progress

Get in the habit of using scaling questions to monitor clients' reports of their progress toward their goals. ("A score of 10 means that you have met your goal for coaching. How close are you to 10 today?")

Although it is tempting to encourage clients to make more and more progress toward 10, at the same time it is important to encourage mastery of the current progress, and not always push to make things better. The ability to maintain the current level of functioning means clients know exactly what to do to keep their cur-

134

rent success. This is important to build clients skills and confidence in their mastery of the ability to make progress. You might also want to have clients scale their confidence that they can maintain their current level. Only when the confidence level seems high enough should you discuss small improvements toward the goal.

Small Increments of Change

There are times when we ask for an increment of 0.5, instead of a full one-point increase either in confidence toward the goal. We learned that some clients, especially those who want to be accurate and precise in everything they do, prefer this kind of detailed measurement. For example, we have met clients who might answer a scaling question by saying, "I would say I am at 4.75" while other clients might say, "I am between 4 and 5." Very different styles—not good or bad, just different. Because we try to match the client's preferred style, it is a good idea for the scales to match it also.

The second occasion to use small increments is when the client's confidence falls on the low end of the scale. We are sensitive about not pushing clients to move faster than they can comfortably navigate. It is not the speed but the fact that the client is making slow but steady improvement that is important.

Many clients and coaches seem to know spontaneously when it is a good time to "stop meeting like this," without spelling it out. Therefore, it is always a good idea to return to the scale during each conversation to keep track of the progress the client is making. When clients reach 7 or 8 consistently on the scale of 1 to 10, most clients and coaches agree that it is time to end the coaching. If the client is uncertain, you can negotiate a trial period when the client could take some time off and then decide whether to return for further sessions. This kind of flexibility on the part of the coach is an excellent service to the client, although it may be hard on the coach's schedule book.

CHAPTER FOUR

COACHING IN CHALLENGING SITUATIONS

Many trainees and seminar participants frequently raise questions about how to work with clients who are viewed as challenging. This label is used to designate and describe multitudes of people and situations. Similar questions are raised frequently during training, consultation, and supervision sessions. In this chapter, we want to present some useful techniques that you can adapt to the unique situations you may face. By discussing experiences with people and situations that are considered challenging, we offer the thinking behind the new strategies and techniques we use. It takes some patience, but these strategies can be mastered.

WE CANNOT MAKE OTHERS CHANGE

Gertrude looked somewhat nervous, not knowing what to expect from a coaching session. A stylish middle-aged woman in her late fifties, Gertrude made an imposing figure. Her eyes were bright and she had an easy smile that projected the air of a gentle grandmother rather than the accountant she said she was. She reported that she had raised two children successfully and they were now in their late twenties. She was looking forward to being a grandmother. She was married to an engineer who was semiretired now and had a busy life pursuing his hobby and nursing his poor health. They took vacations in a warm desert climate during winter months, which was good for his health. When her children were grown and had left home, Gertrude took ceramic classes, and she had become quite good at making garden decoration items that she gave away to family and friends.

Gertrude began describing her work situation in a very methodical manner, saying that she worked for a family-owned construction company that was doing well financially, even in the middle of an economic slump in the field. She began her career as a bookkeeper with the current boss's father, who started the business almost 30 years ago. She was the only employee when he began the company, and now it

> **READER'S EXPERIMENT**
>
> After your next coaching session, take some minutes to reflect:
>
> What have you been doing that was particularly helpful to the client?
>
> What have you managed to do a little bit that you would want to do more of?
>
> What have you not yet done that you would like to try next time in a similar situation?

has grown to employ about 50 people. She was quite distraught and upset at her "junior boss," who she said bullies the employees, including her, and was really ignorant of good business practices and lacked management skills. He yelled and screamed at workers in front of others in the office, called them names, and never apologized when he made a mistake but always blamed others. It was quite obvious that she was very invested in this company, felt personal ties to it, and wanted the workers to be treated well by the boss.

It was not the job that she was complaining about, because she could coast along until retirement, but she became visibly upset and her face flushed with anger and frustration at the junior boss. Every time she described his manners, she almost spat out the "junior" part of her nickname for him, and she became clearly emotional at his "stupidity" and his "temper tantrums." She said the staff were hard-working and good-hearted people. She explained that she was the only person in the company who could scold him and point out his mistakes. He would admit that she was right, only to repeat the same thing. She could not see any lasting changes in his dealings with the staff. We established that her current approach produced momentary regret, but no long-term solution.

As she complained, she made a point of telling me how the junior boss did not have the brains to get through a university program because he was "stupid," and he finally graduated from a lower-ranking community college after many tries. She almost snickered as she told me that now he displayed his diploma in a prominent place in his office as if it were "a diploma from Harvard."

Because of the intensity of her reaction to the junior boss's attitudes and behaviors, it was clear that she needed a sympathetic ear so that she could move on to finding solutions. In an effort to find out what she might consider a useful solution, the coach needed to listen to the effort she had put into helping her boss. The coach learned that her effort was directed at shaming and scolding him to get him to change. Clearly, it was important for her that the young boss treat the workers with dignity. This was where her motivation was; thus, she would be willing to do whatever she could to improve the situation for the workers. Since her enormous effort had not paid off, obviously it was time for Gertrude to do something entirely different.

Listen for Intentions and Efforts

When clients present with this kind of pressing and urgent need to change others, rather than giving a stern lecture on how we cannot change other people, it is helpful to listen to their attempted solutions and good intentions behind their efforts. This helps coaches engaged with clients through the search for solutions to such difficult tasks, especially someone as difficult as Gertrude described. At the same time, it is important for the coach to negotiate the outcome of the session, and the coach can and needs to refocus the conversation on the goal of the session.

Coach: It is very clear that you really care about the workers. You want them to work in a good environment.

Gertrude: Yes, the atmosphere of the company is important, and when he acts in such a stupid way, everybody is unhappy.

Coach: Let me get back to this again. What is your best hope for today's meeting, given how difficult your boss is to work for?

Gertrude: I want him to treat the workers with respect, be nice to them and not yell at them. It creates such a terrible atmosphere at work when he does this. He should listen first and then talk to them calmly. But I don't know if he can learn to do that.

Coach: I am not sure either. Suppose . . . let's just suppose he can learn. What would he say that he would do instead of yelling at the workers?

Gertrude: I hope he would say he will listen to them, but I don't know if he knows how to do that.

Coach: That's a good point. But somehow you must think there is hope for him to change

Gertrude: But if he doesn't change, he will make the company such a difficult place to work and I am afraid that all the good people will leave. Why should these people put up with such a rude boss?

Coach: It is clear that you are very concerned about the future of the company and a good atmosphere for the workers who are there. You obviously care very much about them also.

Gertrude: Yes. That's what worries me the most . . . because it is not good for people to get so upset at work like that. But you know, nobody says anything to him.

Coach: So, what you really want is for the boss to be more thoughtful, mind his manners, and be polite to the workers.

Gertrude: Yes, of course! That's not much to ask. But somehow he just doesn't know that it is a good management policy. People get really upset coming to work because they don't know when he is going to yell at them.

Coach: It occurs to me that you know this company very well. You said you practically watched this junior boss grow up, and then he took over the company from his father. I am curious about one thing you said. What would the boss say is the reason he listens to you when you point out to him what he is doing wrong, even for a short time?

> **HOT TIP**
> The action is in the interaction.

Gertrude: I don't know what he might say, but he knows that I am right, and I am not afraid of him because I can retire anytime. I don't need the job like the other people with young children and a mortgage to pay every month.

Coach: So he knows you are right, that you are not selfish, but you are looking out for the other employees. Is that right?

Gertrude: Yes, he knows that I have been there from the beginning, and he knows that I want what is best for the company and the staff.

Coach: It is quite an accomplishment for you to have conveyed that to him and to have his trust.

Gertrude: Yes, I think so.

Coach: I am curious about one more thing. Knowing this boss as well as you do, what is your own explanation why he is so rude and has such poor manners?

Gertrude: I think he is very insecure inside. He is young and hasn't had much work experience. He inherited this job without the hard work that his father put into it. He just walked into the job because he is the boss's son. So I think he wants to show off that he is the boss.

Coach: That's very interesting. You might be right. Knowing how insecure he is, how helpful would he say it has been to have you point out his mistakes and practically scold him many times?

Gertrude: (*long silence*) Oh, my God! I have never thought about that . . . I have been doing all the wrong things with him!

Conversation Strategies and Techniques That Work

Perhaps a review of the conversation strategies and techniques used with Gertrude might be useful at this point. You might want to think about your own understanding of what steps it took for Gertrude to realize that she had to change her strategies, rather than deciding that her young boss was impossible to work with.

Establish the Client's Good Intention

By repeating this theme several times in the conversation, it was established that Gertrude's intention was honorable and was directed at helping other workers in the company. Also, her long history with the founder of the company established her knowledge of good management practices. Her intention was that this company continue to thrive in tough economic conditions. Her effort to make it a good company to work for was also her way of honoring the original boss who kept her employed for many years.

Maintain Clear Goals

Even in the middle of complaints about others, a coach can always take a few minutes to reestablish and negotiate the goal for the session. Once the coach and the client know the outcome of the conversation, it is easier for the coach to direct the conversation toward what the client wants.

Establish Hope for Change

Because her view is that the boss must change, negotiation with Gertrude about whether it is realistic that he can change is an important reality check. She established that he knows right from wrong and believes that his tolerance of her scolding and shaming him is an indication that he can change. However, part of her complaint is that it is short lived.

Establish the Client's Expertise

In several places in this conversation, the coach was careful to establish Gertrude's expertise, not only on the company and on good management practices, but also on what the workers need and what kind of protection they might need. Most of all, since she took it upon herself to do something about her "stupid" boss, we can easily give her credit for not quietly retiring into a more comfortable life. She is a champion for the workers who are more financially vulnerable than she is.

Clarify the Client's Understanding

All behaviors are based on some rational understanding of what people are trying to accomplish. Therefore, it is important to hear Gertrude's own explanation for the boss's rude behavior. She believes it is because he is "insecure inside."

Expose Solutions that Did Not Work

The client was certainly in the position to do something different with her boss, since her attempts at changing him did not work. When the coach established that her scolding and shaming him did not work, it became possible for Gertrude to search for something else that could increase her chances of success.

Establish the Client's Influence

Making sure Gertrude has a strong influence on the boss and that her intentions are not selfish enhance her motivation to search for a better solution.

Ask What the Target Person Might Want

Most clients are too busy thinking about what the target person is doing wrong. They need to step back and consider what approach might work best with the target person. This not only establishes the client's expertise on the target person but helps the client visualize the next meeting with that person.

Try Something Different

Now Gertrude is ready to entertain a more effective approach to influencing her boss that will make her feel more hopeful, thus beginning a more positive interaction between them. Even a rude boss, especially an insecure one, would respond better to more positive and frequent compliments on what he is doing that is positive already, rather than attempts to stop him from doing something negative.

These strategies may seem complex at first glance, but we suspect that you may be using many of them already in your usually interactions with people, especially with your less difficult clients. The conversation with Gertrude required all of the skills. Being an intelligent and experienced businesswoman, Gertrude had numerous skills that she already used daily with great competence. It might seem overwhelming to think about her situation, but it was quite manageable in brief coaching. Gertrude and the coach met for only two sessions.

If we all wait for someone else to change "because it is his fault," we may have to wait a long time for this insight to translate into behavioral change. No matter whose fault it is, frequently someone with more wisdom and a pragmatic view of life or someone who is in greater discomfort is more likely to step in and initiate change to make things better. Some action is necessary to produce needed changes, no matter who may have caused the problem. There is nothing like a change to produce a difference.

> **TIP FROM THE FIELD**
>
> Invite the client to do something different by asking what would be the simplest thing to start with, and what would be the easiest thing to actually do.

As we have seen with Gertrude and the junior boss, lecturing, or scolding him did not produce the desired change. Giving Elizabeth a stern lecture would have been absolutely useless, since she initially believed that her coworkers were against her and might even be spreading nasty rumors about her. Dismissing Gertrude's concern for other workers at her company as motherly meddling would insult her intelligence and her many years of experience with the company. Both clients could easily have dropped out of coaching, saying that the coach did not really understand them.

DEALING WITH CHALLENGING PEOPLE

When we hear someone describe others as challenging to work with or live with, it usually means the speaker is saying, "I have not figured out how to get along with these difficult others." It does not mean the others are necessarily difficult but the approach being used is not working. What can a coach do with someone who is not in the session but the client sees as the problem? The following are some simple—but not so easy—suggestions that we make.

In most management training, consultation, customer care, and workplace training and coaching sessions, the topic of challenging people comes up quite frequently. One could easily get the impression that companies are full of challenging people who make other people's lives miserable. The good news is that most business management studies indicate that no more than 20% of the people we work with are difficult. In most professional fields, there is a great deal of literature and discussion about difficult, or noncompliant students, patients, workers, and customers. One could easily get the impression that challenging people are rampant, and they are taking over the world. Not so.

What makes it seem that way is that we spend so much of our time and energy thinking about a few difficult people, analyzing them, even evaluating and diagnosing their problems. We try to figure out what might make these people turn around and agree with us and admit their mistakes. Then at a snap of our fingers, they should miraculously turn into different people.

Rather than repeating more of the same steps that did not work, as Gertrude did with her boss, stop what you have been doing right now. Instead, you need to interrupt repetitive patterns that contribute to frustration and unproductive—even destructive—interactions with important people.

Observe What Works

As we described in Chapter 2, all problems have exceptions, times when the familiar problematic pattern did not happen. Pay quiet but careful attention to the interactional pattern between two people, A and B—that is, what A does, then what B does in response to A's behavior, then what A does in response to B's initial response. Most such interactions are predictable and tend to repeat themselves. While you watch for the predictable pattern, at the same time, watch for exceptions that tell you that somehow the two people are breaking the pattern. For some reason, they are doing something slightly different, even for 2 minutes.

We like to begin with a concrete everyday example. In most offices across the world, when people arrive in the morning, they say to their coworkers, "Good morning, how are you today?" Let's imagine two people, Mark and Jim, having this typical conversation. Mark generally is expected to reply, "Oh, good morning, Jim. I'm fine, thanks. It's another gloomy day today. And how are you?" "I'm fine, thanks." This routine or some variation is repeated each day. Nobody thinks of this exchange as problematic because it follows well-accepted and unspoken social rules.

> **HOT QUOTATION**
>
> "Always look at the person's resources first."
>
> —*Insoo Kim Berg*

Observe Reactions Carefully

Suppose that rather than moving on after a brief, routine exchange, Mark decides to break the rule and responds to Jim's morning greeting with details of how he could not sleep the night before, how he had to wake up his wife and tell her that he had an upset stomach, and then goes into detail about what he did, what his wife did, what the children did, and then on top of this, how he came to work later, fighting terrible traffic. After hearing about one of two nights of lost sleep, most people might make a graceful comment about how glad they are to see Mark at work this morning and express hope that he would feel better during the day.

But suppose this continued morning after morning, with Mark repeating the story of his stomach distress, his upset wife, and how his children got on his nerves. After four or five mornings of listening to the gory details of Mark's misery, Jim is most likely to avoid running into Mark. Jim might even stay inside his office, with the door closed, thus avoiding the now inevitable pattern of Mark going on about his troubles, making Jim feel helpless to do anything about it. Now a new pattern of avoiding the person who breaks social rules is established. So what do these rules have to do with coaches?

Pattern Interruption

By refusing to engage in repetitive morning conversation with Mark, Jim has learned to interrupt the pattern that makes him uncomfortable. For the time being, Jim's annoyance at Mark's disregard of social rules is resolved. However, imagine you are faced with someone like Mark, and you cannot avoid him for the rest of the day because either you share an office with Mark, or Mark is your boss and you are reluctant to jeopardize your working relationship with him. What can you do?

Jim may feel like changing jobs, or ask to have his office moved, or make other changes so that he is not likely to run into Mark every morning. It does not contribute to a good working relationship between Jim and Mark if one person feels put upon or victimized by the other. Because we advocate trying small changes first, we suggest replacing the familiar pattern with the following different interactions.

What

Look into the possibility of changing what Jim does in response to Mark's daily recitation of his misery. For example, changes can begin with the question "How are you?" Jim could replace the typical morning ritual with political news of the day, football game scores, or tales of a snowstorm or flood somewhere in the world, or an interesting cooking show he watched the night before on television. Or he may want to bring up a topic that he heard on his car radio during your morning commute. You can imagine how it might force Mark to respond if Jim selected such a topic, thus creating a possibility that they may engage in a different type of morning conversation.

Where

Can the interaction take place somewhere other than the familiar spot next to the coffee machine or at the office door? Experiment with changing the location where nonproductive conversation occurs. The more unexpected, the better, not only because of the element of surprise but also because the spontaneous interaction can produce some surprisingly positive results. The change of location can actually change the topic of the conversation. Many corporate meetings, conferences, and other important meetings take place in a setting that is conducive to an enhanced atmosphere.

Who

Changing who is involved in the interaction can produce different results. Jim may want to talk to Judy first in the morning, instead of always talking to Mark first. Having Judy join in the conversation may bring in some new perspective and patterns and possibly could lead to some unexpected directions, and thus unknown solutions.

When

As people often say, "Timing is everything." Indeed, when Jim decides to talk to Mark could make a world of difference. Therefore, Jim should experiment with talking to Mark at a different time of the morning or even in the afternoon. Thus the topic will change.

How

There is a famous story about Milton Erickson, who was a genius at pattern interruption with difficult patients. But this story involves an experiment he conducted on a busy sidewalk. Erickson walked down the crowded street of a busy city, and someone rushing from the opposite direction bumped into him, practically knocking him over. Without an apology he began to rush on. Erickson made an elaborate gesture of stretching out his left arm as if to look at his watch to see what time it was. He immediately said loudly to the man who bumped into him, "Young man, it is exactly 2 o'clock" and moved on a few steps. A few seconds later he turned around and saw the young man stopped dead in his tracks, still looking at Erickson with a confused and puzzled expression. This kind of totally unexpected and out-of-the-blue response can turn a familiar interactional pattern around. This is an example of a pattern interruption, that is, doing something totally unexpected so that the other person is forced to behave in a totally different manner.

We want to emphasize that frequently changing any of the elements of the interactional pattern is enough. However, more difficult problems call for different strategies.

The Smallest, Easiest, and Simplest Change

Again, the temptation is to try to change everything because by the time clients find a situation so unbearable that they bring it to a coach's attention, clients are ready to overdo it and try everything they have ever heard of. Doing too many things at the same time may make one feel better for a short while, but it is difficult to know which efforts worked and which did not. Therefore, it is always a good idea to try something small, simple, and easy first, then try something else, and then see which solution works the best.

To go back to Gertrude, the coach can help her look for the smallest, simplest behavioral changes in her boss. A coach can help Gertrude notice small differences that might be the beginning of a solution for her.

Case Examples

The following case examples illustrate creative ways to achieve a pattern interruption.

Business Sense and the Organized Desk

Mr. Schneider was a buyer for a women's clothing wholesale store and his job required him to travel on various buying trips. He had to rely heavily on his assistant, Henrietta, to help him run the business side of his job. Mr. Schneider was very frustrated with Henrietta. He explained that she often ignored phone calls and e-mails from potential customers, although she was always busy and very good at organizing files. Her desk was always neat, and the account books were updated and accurate, but she ignored potential sales calls and would only leave a message for him about who called with a number to call back. He wanted her to have more business sense and not just be a keeper of neat files.

The coach asked Mr. Schneider what might be the smallest sign that would tell him that Henrietta was beginning to develop business sense. Mr. Schneider had a great deal of difficulty with this question initially. After much help from the coach, he finally described it as her ability to tell which phone calls indicated potential sales and which did not, instead of handing him a message about who called.

Later, Mr. Schneider called to report his surprise after returning to his office. As soon as he returned from the coaching session, Henrietta handed him a message from a potential customer with a note saying, "Mr. Cooper called and it might develop into a big sale." He was astonished.

How did this happen? It is very possible that Henrietta had done this before, but until Mr. Schneider had to really sit down and think about what exactly he wanted his assistant to do, he may not have noticed what Henrietta was doing to indicate that she had the beginning of business sense. Now that he knew exactly what he wanted Henrietta to do, he was able to see it better for the first time. Now he was able to support and encourage Henrietta to develop further business sense.

It is important to remember not to try something out of anger or malice, but to assume the good intentions of others until proven otherwise. We have no idea what someone is thinking until we ask and find out. Therefore, even in frustrating situations, we cannot go wrong by beginning with an assumption that others are motivated by good intentions. If we learn otherwise, we will always have time to change course. We also do not know what ideas Henrietta might have on how being orderly and organized might be related to business sense. Should Mr. Schneider decide to ask Henrietta, he might learn some surprising things.

A Subtle Suggestion

A good colleague of ours, David, is a school psychologist. His office faced directly across from the classroom of a fifth grade teacher who yelled and screamed at her class all day long so loudly that when his office door was open, he could hear every word she spewed at the children. Not only it was disturbing David's concentration, but he was very concerned about the children who were subjected to her loud, harsh voice all day long in the classroom. The school rule was that all classroom doors were to be left open throughout the day to promote openness. Parents, visitors, and administrators were free to walk around the hallways and observe what the students and teachers were doing.

David wanted to do something to interrupt the teacher's harsh tone, but he did not have the authority to talk to her directly because he was not her superior. He thought and thought about this situation and decided that he needed to do something different than most people would.

He decided to be friendly with the teacher first. He made a point of talking to her during lunch hour, got her to make small talk, and learned about her personal life and living situation. One day, the conversation took a turn to music and their dreams early in life. David asked the teacher whether she ever took voice lessons while she was growing up. To his surprise and shock, she said yes, she took voice lessons and her aspiration was to be an opera star. Of course, he became very interested in her voice training and asked lots of questions that any novice or untrained person would ask. The teacher eagerly provided David with lots of information about her voice training days and how to produce certain sounds and so on. Of course, the more curious he became, the more animated she became in explaining all the fine points of voice training and breathing techniques.

> **QUESTION FROM THE FIELD**
>
> "If the boss is paying for the coaching, how do you include the boss's goals in the coaching conversation?"
>
> A very simple and effective way to include the interests of third parties is to adapt your coaching questions: "What would need to happen here today so that you and your boss would say that it has been a useful session?"

To his pleasant surprise, the teacher's voice became softer and softer as weeks went by, and her wonderful singer's voice became more gentle. The pleasant side effect was that they became good friends and David discovered that the teacher was quite a nice person.

What did David do to get the teacher to use a softer voice with children? Our understanding is that David did a number of things that any coach can easily adapt to their situation with clients.

- David was able to set aside his internal criticism of the teacher and became interested in her: her interests, her social life, her passion. He showed interest in her as a person first, not only as a teacher.
- David was looking for any strength or area of competence that she had. Because he wanted her to use a softer voice with children, his thoughts went in the direction of asking about voice lessons or interest in music.
- It was an unexpected, surprising stroke of good luck that indeed the teacher had voice training in her younger day.
- By directing his conversation to her area of expertise, David was able to direct the teacher's attention to the good use of her voice, without saying a word about her screeching.

- Sometimes, subtle suggestions to clients work better than directly pointing out their mistakes. They do not encourage defensiveness in the other person.

The Power of Compliments

A coach was asked to give three lectures on communications training to a group of highway road repair workers. The lectures were scheduled for 3 days spread over 2 months because the workers could not take 3 days off. The workers did not ask for this training, but management and the labor union negotiated that training on communication would help reduce the number of sexual harassment complaints. More and more women workers were entering the job market in this area which predominantly employed men.

The coach specialized in sexual harassment laws in the workplace and much of her class material involved accurate communication between male and female workers to reduce the frequency of sexual harassment episodes. Sexual harassment complaints can result in bruising and bitter disputes among workers and can leave a long-lasting undercurrent of resentment. Such lawsuits are costly, not only financially but also in terms of worker morale and lost productivity. Therefore, management decided that this was crucial training that everybody needed.

Some workers were resentful of having to sit through "sissy talk" about communication, beside the fact that this was the first time they had to learn from a female instructor. Gary, a particularly outspoken young man, was extremely critical of the instructor and made frequent references to inside jokes and used suggestive language. The entire class would laugh along with him. It was clear that Gary was enjoying making her feel uncomfortable during the first day of training. She felt insulted and disrespected by this young man who continuously berated her, and nobody in the class came to her defense or told him to behave better.

The coach lost her self-control and blew up at Gary at the end of the day. She told him that he was rude and she was not forcing him to sit through the class. If he wanted, would he please leave and let the others learn what they came to learn? It was a totally unexpected outburst, and the coach felt terrible about it afterward. She felt at a loss to know how she could regain her position, as she had two more days of training with the entire class.

The coach thought about this unusual episode and decided that there was nothing she could do about what happened that day. She would have to take a step that could be educational for Gary as well as to recover from embarrassment herself. At the beginning of the next lecture, the coach told Gary in front of the class that she had been thinking about what happened the day before, and she came to realize that she made a big mistake in not recognizing what an enormous amount of courage Gary showed by being so willing to speak up the day before. She told him that she was impressed by his independence and willingness to risk his reputation by speaking out honestly about his assessment of the class and how much she appreciated his willingness to stand up for his beliefs. Then she dropped the subject and never mentioned it again and made sure that she was fair with Gary for the rest of the two remaining days.

To her surprise, at the end of the last training day Gary stood up and told everyone how surprised he was that he learned so much about communication, workplace ethics, and respect for women. He was surprised at how much he learned from this class, including the teacher who had the guts to apologize in public. He thanked the coach for having taught him how important listening was in communication. We want to emphasize that the use of compliments is not limited to coaching only.

CLIENTS IN CONFLICT

Conflict or disagreement between people is inevitable in most setting where two or more people work or live together. In coaching, you are most likely to work with one partner in conflict with someone else who is not present in the session. However, sometimes two partners in conflict may seek your help together. You may decide to meet with both partners in the disagreement to be efficient and solve problems quickly. Therefore, it is good to know how to manage both situations. In this section, we first address how to work with one person who is in conflict with someone else who is not present in the session. Then we turn our attention to how to organize your sessions when two people in conflict request your services.

Working With One Person in Conflict

As is true with most coaching conversations, the first conversation always begins with goals or the positive outcome the client is seeking. It is helpful to remember that there is no one right way

TIP FROM THE FIELD

Scaling questions can help to speed up solution finding in conflict situations:

Ask both parties to position their conflict and goal on a scale from 1 to 10, 1 being the worst the conflict has ever been and 10 being the ultimate goal:

What would you be doing differently at 10?

Where would you say things are right now?

How far do you want to get in this session?

What would you be doing being that you are not yet doing, if you were one point higher on the scale?

Talking about progress on the scale is a very effective way to stay at the surface moving toward solutions. Lengthy discussions about the origins and details of the conflict usually do not help but make things worse.

to manage the conflict. It will depend on the circumstances and the context of the conflict, and on the realistic outcome that clients believe will make life a little bit better. Ask questions such as these: "Suppose you agree on the best path to pursue. What would you be doing then that you are not doing now?" "Knowing your partner as well as you do, what would your partner say needs to happen here so that this conversation will be helpful for both of you?"

Staying Neutral

One of the most difficult aspects of working with persons in conflict is the natural tendency to experience pressure to take sides, either by coaches' internal feelings or the participants' desire to have their position validated and supported. Being supportive of each person's position is not the same as supporting and encouraging positions that have not produced cooperation or collaboration. Of course, everybody needs and wants support and validation that they are on the right track. It takes skill to accept both viewpoints without supporting or approving ideas that may not work.

Many coaches have mistaken notions that we cannot support both sides at the same time, but clients appreciate fair and honest feedback from a coach and they can distinguish whether you are biased toward one party or the other. What should you do? You could say, "Yes, of course, I can see how you have come to this conclusion, Mr. Brown, but I can also see, Ms. White, how you can view it in a different way." Or try this: "I can see both of you disagree on how to proceed from here on. I wonder if there is a way to combine both of your ideas and come to a third way of looking at it." Staying neutral and being fair-minded is crucial to the negotiation process. This is a coach's most important value to clients.

Useful Tools

The most useful tool at this stage of negotiation is to bring the voice or perception of the absent party into the conversation by using relationship questions, such as these:

- What do you suppose your boss would way needs to happen here so that he would believe it was a good idea to pay for coaching for you?
- What would your team members say that shows they could tell that you are beginning to make useful contributions to the team's effort?
- Suppose your staff believes that you are more fair with all of them, instead of believing that you favor certain staff members. What would they see you doing differently that would tell them that you are beginning to listen them?

- Suppose your colleagues communicate with you more about their plans regarding this project. What would they see you do then that you are not doing right now? What else?
- Suppose your manager recognizes the important contribution you are making this project. What would he do then that he is not doing right now? What else?
- Suppose that team spirit moves up on the same scale of 1 to 10. What would they say that you will do to give them credit for doing a good job?
- What would change then in team morale? What else?

Perception Is Reality

Even though the other participant in the client's conflict may not be present, what the client perceives and believes about the other person is very real to the client. It is not our job to judge whether the client's perception is accurate or not, because we are not there to judge who is right or wrong but to change the client's perception slightly so that different responses are possible. Yet, what the client believes is very real and he or she will behave as if it is real. Therefore, accepting the client's perception and working with this reality makes it easier to bring the absent person's perception into the conversation to offer a more balanced view.

Contrary to most coaches' fears, we find that clients are surprisingly accurate in their perception of what the other person might say and do because they interact with each other almost daily and probably have had many discussions or arguments with each other. When we work with the client's view of the situation, we are not taking sides with either party in the conflict. Instead, we empower the client to be the first person to find solutions, rather than dwelling on and suffering from the problem. For example, consider the following short conversation with a young chef who felt that she had been passed over for a promotion even though she had tremendous feedback when she managed the executive dining room for a year. She felt slighted that her boss did not recognize her cooking talents and the artistic and creative work she did for the executives of the company.

Coach: Suppose I ask your boss what he appreciates the most about your work as the executive dining room chef. Any idea about what he would say?

Client: I suppose he would say that I was very sensitive about balancing the healthy menu with artistic expression in my cooking. I love having room to be creative with what I do. The executives know and appreciate good food and the CEO came up to me and congratulated me on my cooking in front of others, even my boss.

Coach: I am sure you are very creative with your cooking. So what would your boss say he would like to see you become better at?

Client: He might say I need to get along better with other chefs, like the pastry chef. I can't stand him and he is always showing off. I know I need to have better people skills, specially with him. Everybody in the kitchen always watches what kind of mood I am in, whether I am going to explode that day or not.

Coach: What would your boss say he would like to see you change by coming to coaching?

Client: He would definitely say that I need to have stable moods. That's always the issue with me. I know I need to control my emotions so that I can get along with others.

Coach: When you learn to control your emotions better, who would be the first to notice that you are doing it?

Client: The kitchen crew would not be watching to see what kind of mood I am in when I get to work early in the morning.

Coach: So what would they see in you instead?

Client: They would see me smiling more, being more friendly, and handling my frustrations better, so that I don't upset the smooth running of the kitchen.

Coach: Suppose you are more stable and handle your emotions better. What would your boss notice about you that he does not see now?

Client: He would see me smiling more, talking to other staff, being friendly with them, and being more confident that they do not have to be afraid of me.

Who Is Motivated to Change?

In most coaching situations, a coach is more likely to work with the person who is most motivated to change the relationship. This person either stands to lose the most if the conflict is not resolved or feels the most discomfort and therefore is willing to change the pattern to restore harmony in the workplace. Working with one person who is motivated for a variety of reasons can make the coaching process move very quickly. You can use any number of the various tools presented in Chapter 2.

> **QUESTION FROM THE FIELD**
> "Do you follow up on conflict situations between two people?"
>
> We have found it useful to schedule a follow-up session. During the follow-up session, you get to reinforce helpful things clients have been doing, and you can normalize ups and downs they have encountered. Ask both parties:
>
> On a scale of 1 to 10, where would you say you have been this past week?
>
> What did you see happen that makes you say you are already at x and not lower?
>
> How can you maintain the progress that you have made?

Working With Two Parties in Conflict

A successful owner of a medium-sized printing company, Mr. Mundt, requested help from a coach because he felt such intense pressure from two of his top employees who were constantly trying to one-up each other. They were both hard-working, bright, and motivated and he wanted to keep both of them. One difficulty was that each one came to him complaining about the other. One was an ambitious and attractive young woman who definitely was a rising star. He wanted to mentor and nurture her potential to rise in his company to show the business community that he was in step with the changing times. The other employee was a young man who was willing to stay late at work and had some very creative and innovate ideas to take the company to the next level. Both would come to him complaining about mistakes the other made and at times they accused each other of deliberately making the other look bad. At first Mr. Mundt tolerated it as creative competitiveness, but lately he found himself spending more and more time and energy thinking and talking to these two.

The next step depends a great deal on the outcome negotiation: Does he want to learn how to solve this tough situation on his own? Does he want the coach to take over mediating the disputes between these employees? In either approach, what is his goal for these two employees? What does he need to see these employees do to get the idea that working with a coach has been successful? In addition, does he want to learn so that this kind of problem does not happen again in his company? Mr. Mundt decided that he did not have time to learn to manage these employees, and he asked the coach to help them both. After the tension was resolved, he wanted to talk to the coach again about how to make sure that his kind of problem did not happen again in his company.

When you observe two people in conflict, it can make you feel overwhelmed and wonder how you can be helpful. The reason for this intense discomfort is that we often feel like we are called upon to become judges. We feel the pressure to make a decision about who is right and wrong. Observing people in intense conflict can also elicit quite uncomfortable feelings and may make you feel like you want to run away, or quickly give them a right answer. Yet those in conflict need our help more than anyone because conflict can be quite destructive and can easily spread to other areas of the organization.

Common Goals

Most disagreements and disputes are about how to get from here to there, and often the parties lose sight of where they want to go. In other words, the disputes often are about the methods of how to get from point A to point B. To look at this another way, should they ride bicycles or horses, roller-skate, drive a car, use a sail-boat, or ride a train to get form here to there.

Therefore, the immediate goal is to determine what kind of concrete outcome they both want. Mr. Mundt's decision was to have someone else help the employees so that they could return to being more productive again. This was the boss's mandate; now the coach needed to find out what both employees wanted to achieve from their "mandated" participation in coaching. Recognizing

QUESTION FROM THE FIELD

"Often the person or organization that initiated the coaching wants to be kept informed about the progress of the coaching. How do you do that without breaking confidentiality with the client?"

What we have found to work is just reporting the number on the progress scale. Of course we ask clients' permission to pass on this answer for each session. Sometimes we encourage clients to report back directly to the initiator whatever they think is appropriate. If it is possible, from time to time we schedule three-way meetings where we can ask the initiators what changes for the better they have noticed. This can be very reinforcing for the client.

this, the coach began with compliments on how their boss must value them both enough that he wanted to spend the money, time, and energy to select a coach for them, along with using company time so that they would work as a team. Even though they tried to blame each other, reciting many details of their grievances against each other, the coach had to firmly redirect the conversation and repeatedly remind them that what the coach wanted to learn was what their boss saw in them that told him that they were worth the investment of money and time. Also, the coach wanted to know what the boss wanted them to accomplish through coaching. Both Jocelyn and Brian, after considerable effort, finally agreed that they wanted to get along with each other so that they could become a true team. Each wanted the other to contribute to their cooperation.

Details of Solutions

The coaching conversation was about what each would do when they get along and how Mr. Mundt would be able to tell that they were getting along. Because Mr. Mundt is an integral part of their conflict, it is important that the coaching conversation must continue to refer to his goals. The concrete signs of solutions included Brian and Jocelyn not running to their boss to complain about each other, even though they felt like doing it. First they would walk away for a few minutes to think it over. Each would be able to give the other person credit when one thought that the other person did a good job. The other employees' perception of the changes between the two were discussed as well. The coach agreed with Mr. Mundt that when two people make their working relationship more positive, they can have a tremendous influence on other employees as well because their positive energy will spill into other aspects of the company. Listen to all the things the coach heard from Jocelyn and Brian. Notice how the coach focused on certain comments and ignored other interactions between the two.

Coach: Before we start, I am curious about what your boss, Mr. Mundt, sees in both of your contributions to the company that makes him want to go out of his way to make sure that you two get along well. Obviously he must see a great deal of potential in both of you.

Jocelyn: I guess so. I have not thought about it that way, but yes, I guess so.

Brian: Yes, I will have to agree with Jocelyn on that. I have been with the company slightly longer than Jocelyn and I suppose he sees me working long hours and giving all I have to help the company grow.

Jocelyn: I may be a little bit newer in the company, but I think Mr. Mundt sees me as energetic, hard-working, and a fast learner.

Coach: I am sure you both have a lot to offer the company. I am curious about what outcome each of you would like to see happen as a result of our talking together today?

Jocelyn: What Mr. Mundt told me was that he values my contribution to the company and he would like to see me continue with the company, but he insisted that Brian and I must become a team.

Brian: Yes . . . he told me the same thing. Becoming a team is a good idea but . . .

Coach: Suppose you become a team. What would Mr. Mundt see the two of you doing that he does not see right now?

As you might normally do with individual clients, it is also important to begin with client strengths and competencies and acknowledging their boss's investment in their success in coaching. At the same time, it is crucial not to get distracted by Jocelyn's move to outdo Brian or by their competitiveness with each other. Keeping the focus on the common goal is the first priority in such a situation. At the same time, since both were sent by their boss, Mr. Mundt's criteria for a successful outcome must be addressed first. In a situation such as this, there are three clients to pay attention to. That is, Mr. Mundt identified his desired solutions, but because Jocelyn and Brian are the ones that must implement the solutions, the coach needs to pay close attention to how they would need to cooperate so that solutions can be identified and carried out. This approach makes it possible for all three people to invest in a successful outcome. Observe how Mr. Mundt's goals are woven into the conversation here.

> **QUESTION FROM THE FIELD**
> "How do you keep from ending up doing the manager's job of communicating with the employee?"
>
> The best way we have come up with is to schedule an initial meeting where both parties involved talk about what they want out of the coaching, so that the messages can be heard directly, and the coach can avoid becoming a messenger for either side.

Jocelyn: I guess the most important sign is that we will come to him less often, or not at all, and still get our work done.

Brian: I would agree with that. I realize that we must look like two kids fighting with each other and running to Daddy to mediate our fights. I guess what would be the most significant indication to him is that we are learning to be a team. We shouldn't run to him each time we disagree.

Coach: OK, sounds very reasonable. So what would Mr. Mundt see you two doing instead of running to him to mediate your disagreements?

Jocelyn: I guess he would see us meeting with each other often without him on various projects.

Coach: So somehow you learn to become a team and work on a project together without his mediation. How would he find out that you are a team now?

Brian: I suppose we would report to him about decisions we make and get his approval on implementation steps and cost estimates.

Coach: Sounds like a very good idea. I'm impressed. What would it take for you to become a team without Mr. Mundt's help?

Jocelyn: I guess I will have to call a meeting since I am the customer service manager.

Coach: OK, suppose you call a meeting with Brian. What would you do that will signal to Brian that you are really interested in working with him this time?

Jocelyn: I don't know. . . . I haven't thought about it . . . but I suppose I will use a friendly voice and ask him to meet instead of demanding . . . maybe even walk over to his office . . . something like that.

Brian: Yeah, I would appreciate that very much.

Coach: So, Jocelyn, when you ask for a meeting instead of demanding, talk to Brian in a friendly tone of voice, walk over to his office, and so on, what would you see Brian doing to show you that he wants to be a team with you?

Jocelyn: I will see him smiling at me, and he will use a friendly tone of voice instead of the gruff voice he uses sometimes. He will give me a response right away, instead of putting me off by saying how busy he is.

Coach: Can either of you tell me when was the most recent time that you had a conversation that told you that you are a team? Any idea about that?

Brian: I don't know. . . . It's been a long time, it seems . . . maybe I would say about a month or so ago. It was a rush job. The customer was in such a hurry and it was a big order, too, so we knew that we didn't want to lose the business. We really forgot about our usual fight and just pitched in and got the stuff done to meet the customer's deadline. I think he is still our customer because we helped him out when he was in a tough spot. I guess somebody quit on him or something like that.

Jocelyn: Yeah, I remember that customer. I think he's in a food catering business, if I remember correctly.

Coach: I wonder how that happened. Very interesting. It tells me that you can become a team. I can see why Mr. Mundt was so interested in keeping both of you. It makes sense.

Notice that when Jocelyn offers indications of successful teamwork that Mr. Mundt will notice, both Jocelyn and Brian are forced to step out of their own point of view and look at themselves from their boss's perspective. Thus, when Jocelyn offers a good idea, Brian is compelled to either agree with her or come up with even better solutions. Because both are extremely ambitious and motivated, it is natural that they are competitive, which in itself is a good thing for an organization. Well-managed competitiveness can be a positive force in most organizations. However, competitiveness can turn destructive. Therefore, the coach can help turn their competitive nature into a positive force—they can compete to see who will become a better team member. Once the goal is established, the conversation can continue with more detailed description of this teamwork. Of course, the more they become a team, the more they will come to appreciate each other's contributions. They will be able to move to the next phase of their teamwork, either with or without the coach's assistance.

A coach can ask about exceptions as soon as the partners in the session can agree on the desirable outcome or if they can answer the miracle question with a concrete, behavioral description of the exception in detail. Once the goal is clear so that all three participants will recognize the small desired changes, then the simplest and easiest next step is to find out about the times when they behave like team members and how Mr. Mundt could tell that they are a team without either of them informing him. Once the common goal is described in a realistic, concrete way, the rest of the work with two people can be fun. When more than one person is marching toward the same goal, especially with a history of working together and commitment to improve the productivity of an organization, it can be an awesome experience for a coach.

Ending the Contact

All later sessions would follow a similar format— keeping track of what is getting better, even for a short time, and encouraging the clients to keep doing what works. Depending on what kind of contract Mr. Mundt has, a coach can use a scaling question to find out how satisfied Mr. Mundt is with the progress his employees are making in becoming a team.

MANDATED CLIENTS

Some coaches believe that clients who come to coaching involuntarily, or are mandated to come at the risk of losing their jobs, for example, are difficult to work with. We disagree. There are some initial useful strategies that a coach needs to know; however, once engaged properly in the client's own agenda, the actual work is not all that difficult. In fact, such mandated clients can turn out to be quite successful and you may be able to establish a reputation for working with difficult clients. The following are some guidelines for coaches to remember.

> **TIP FROM THE FIELD**
>
> When working to motivate mandated clients, ask about the positive consequences of reaching their goals. Give them time to reflect on what makes goals attractive and important to them.

Confidentiality

Most coaching is negotiated with clients who request your services for themselves, therefore, many things relate to the service with the client directly, including confidentiality of information related to the client.

However, when an employee is referred, it usually means the employer who refers the client will pay for the service. Therefore, it is important for you to negotiate clearly what kind of information the employer expects from you. If your agreement with the employer is that you will bill the employer, make sure that information will be limited to the number of times you met. Once this is done, then you need to inform the client about this understanding.

Self-Check

If you have any bias or misconceptions about mandated clients, make sure you check them at the door and do not let them interfere with what you need to do with your client. Such clients frequently come to you with referral information, usually from managers who have not found ways to cooperate with them. Therefore, you may hear many negative things about the client from a frustrated manager. Make sure you let your curiosity be your guide, not your prejudice about the label.

Engage With the Person First, Not the Problem

Rather than being concerned about the problem, connect with the person first. That is, many coaches make the mistake of seeing the problem first, then the person who is attached to the problem. This mistake is guaranteed to make your work with the person very difficult. Find out about clients' interests, competencies, successes, accomplishments that they might be proud of, and so on that tell us about them.

Learn What Is Important to the Person

Since the changes the employer wants from coaching must be carried out by the employee, and, as we articulated earlier, we cannot force someone to change, it is important to find out what is important enough for the client that he or she would be willing to do what it takes to implement the necessary changes. So far, it is quite similar to working with voluntary clients. At times, what the employer wants and what the worker wants from coaching may not be the same. Again, since the employee is the person who needs to do something to make the necessary changes, it is important to listen to what is important to the employee. The following questions may be useful:

Coach: What would the boss need to see happen here for you so that she would say this coaching has been useful to you?

Employee: I suppose she wants me to come to work on time every day. But you know it is very difficult to do when I have to rely on my babysitter to come to my house before I can leave the children. I cannot leave my young children alone just because I have to go to work.

Coach: Suppose you find a way to get to work on time every day. What would be different between you and your manager?

Employee: I suppose she would become calm and not so worried that I may not show up for work.

Coach: Suppose your manager is calm and not so worried. What would change between you and her?

Employee: Well, she would get off my back and not watch me all the time. She would leave me alone and not check up on me.

Coach: When she gets off your back and doesn't watch you all the time, what difference would it make for you?

Employee: I would be calmer and I could get my work done better because I would not be so stressed out. I think her watching me is more stressful than the work. I like the work but I feel like I am under a microscope and I have to watch everything I do. It would be nice not to feel that pressure.

Since the stress point is her relationship with her manager, what is important is for the manager to leave her alone and she would likely be more productive on the job. Therefore, both the employee and the manager would benefit.

Learn Who Is Important to the Person

Frequently, learning about who the client depends on, or who is motivated to do certain things, or is supportive of the client, and has influence over the client can be a tremendous resource for the client.

Find Out What the Client Can Do

The first rule of generating solutions is to enhance what clients already know how to do, that is, their existing abilities and competencies. We want to utilize these competencies and build more successful skills, rather than eliminating undesirable traits. This is the best way we know to generate rapid changes. We also believe this is the most respectful way of working with someone who was forced to come and talk to us. It reduces their reluctance to talk to us.

Find out what the client is willing to do. Clearly, if something is important to the client, he or she is more likely to want to act to make changes. Rather than trying to push a river uphill, which is an impossible task, we want to learn where the river is likely to flow and then follow the flow. We are saying to the river that we respect

> **QUESTION FROM THE FIELD**
>
> "I have had mandated clients who say they have already accomplished their goals and have done everything asked of them. Should I confront them with the initiator's perception that this isn't true?"
>
> We have learned that if we directly confront mandated clients, they will usually dig in their heels and resist our efforts to make progress. Challenge them to become aware of their own process of change. When clients say they have learned their lesson, we ask, "How do you know that?" "How can your employer tell that you have learned your lesson?" We follow up with more questions asking for details.

and appreciate the function and beauty of the river, and we are not out to change the course of the river drastically.

Learn the Client's Desired Outcome

Clearly, we want to help create a solution that is sustainable and long lasting, not a temporary fix that will revert back to the original condition as soon as coaching is over. This phase of goal negotiation is quite similar to working with voluntary clients. Because all this sounds rather academic, we want to describe how these things are accomplished at the practice level by describing the example of Mr. Henry.

"They Aren't Like they Used to Be"

Mr. Henry was in his mid-50s, with graying hair. He sat slumped in the waiting area, clearly not happy to be in a coach's office. He barely managed to be polite but carried on a conversation as best he could. He explained that he had been a high school science teacher and track coach for "too many years," indicating that he was pretty bored with teaching and that he had no idea why he was at the coach's office.

Because he was not going to bring it up, the coach initiated the conversation by saying that she was very impressed with how highly his boss must think of Mr.

Henry to call her personally and wanted her to talk to him. He grunted an agreement, indicating that he did not think much of the principal. The coach tried to engage him in small talk about his teaching career and he answered as briefly as possible, without elaborating much.

Coach: I understand that you are a good science teacher, and you won an award as the best science teacher in the city.

Mr. Henry: Yeah, but that was a long time ago. Kids are different these days.

Coach: I also understand that you are a track coach.

Mr. Henry: Yeah, for many years.

Coach: I realize that being here is not your idea of how to spend your time. What do you think your principal would like to see come out of this meeting today?

Mr. Henry: I have nothing against you, but I really don't think I belong here.

Coach: Perhaps not. I am interested in learning about what makes your boss willing to go out of her way to make sure that you get back to the top form that apparently you had in the past. Any idea?

Mr. Henry: I suppose she thinks I should be nicer to kids and their parents. I guess she does not want to hear any complaints about me from the parents and students. But kids have no respect for teachers and their parents are too busy making money. Kids are left on their own these days. They are not like they used to be, you know.

Coach: I am not sure about that. Suppose somehow they learn to be more respectful of you and parents are more concerned about their children. What would your principal say that she will see different about you?

185

Even though Mr. Henry did not appear cooperative in the beginning, the fact that he kept the appointment and responded to each question, even though reluctantly, indicates a degree of hope that he could be engaged. Therefore, it was important for the coach to show respect for his achievements and give him credit for his past successes and accomplishments. The principal's mandate that Mr. Henry get coaching help was framed as her investment in Mr. Henry, even though it appeared that Mr. Henry resented being told to show up for an appointment with a coach.

Even though Mr. Henry made outrageous statements about children and their parents these days, the coach did not need to point them out or confront him about this yet because confrontation rarely works and it was too early to dispute his opinion. Notice how frequent use of tentative language worked well with Mr. Henry. Because the referral was from the principal, the coach needed to take into account the principal's goal as a major concern. The coach's first task was to engage with the client and negotiate a goal and what the client was willing and able to do to make the needed changes, as well as helping him see how it might benefit him.

Mr. Henry: I suppose she would say I would go back to the way I was when I had a passion for teaching. In my earlier years.

Coach: How long ago are we talking about? I mean, when you had a passion for teaching?

Mr. Henry: I am not sure. I guess my life slowly shriveled up and disappeared . . . maybe three or four years. . . . I'm not sure.

Coach: Suppose I ask some of your students from those days what you were like then as a teacher. What would they tell me they appreciated most about you?

Mr. Henry: I think they might say I cared about them, that I went out of my way and really cared about them, their learning, and their future, what was going on in their families, and things like that. You know, my wife says the same thing, that I should be more interested in my students.

Coach: What would your former students say was different about you from other teachers that made you the best teacher of the year?

Mr. Henry: I suppose they would say I was patient with them, cared about them, and it showed without my saying it in so many words. I was willing to listen to them, I suppose. I guess I have no patience anymore for the stupid stuff they do these days.

Coach: So what did the students do to show you that they appreciated your patience and that you cared about them? How could you tell in those days?

Mr. Henry: They would catch me in the hallways and joke with me. They would drop in my office and talk to me about their personal problems. Even after graduation, the kids would drop in when they were in town and tell me about what they were doing in college, stuff like that. Of course I had to be a father figure to some kids who did not have their fathers living with them.

Coach: Would you say those were the days when you had a passion for teaching?

Mr. Henry: Yeah, I guess so. I really cared about them. After I had a mild heart attack 4 or 5 years ago, I guess I just withdrew and avoided the kids and my teaching became a burden, instead of a passion.

Coach: What would it take to get your passion back?

Mr. Henry: Gee, I don't know. My wife says I got old all of a sudden.

Coach: Suppose you get your passion back. What would you be doing then that you are not doing right now?

Mr. Henry: My wife says I should get back to playing golf, being more active. I had a passion for Celtic music, you know. I have Irish blood in me.

TIP FROM THE FIELD

In the beginning stage of coaching, mandated clients never take the high moral ground by arguing in favor of making prudent (in your view) changes. When the coach begins to argue in favor of change, the client can only argue against it. How can you tell you are arguing with the client? A sure sign is when you find yourself saying, "Yes, but" or simply "But ..." However, you can help clients see the advantages of making some changes by enouraging them to stay the same.

As the conversation continued, Mr. Henry volunteered more and more information about himself within a short time. The longer they talked about Mr. Henry's picture of his passion for teaching, the more animated and excited he got about talking about the old days. Without having to articulate his goals for coaching, the conversation was deliberately focused on his successful days of teaching and ways to get his passion back. The same principle of listening for client resources, past successes, and what the client might want is particularly important for mandated clients because many of them have no expectation that coming to talk to a coach will benefit them in any way.

Once you get a sense that the client is interested in the future, and the detailed road map unfolds, the client becomes engaged in looking for solutions. After that, the rest of the contact can be quite similar to any other case. The presence of Mr. Henry's boss, his wife, and his current students will all play supporting roles in future conversations.

INDECISIVE CLIENTS

Many clients bring to coaching their need to make a good decision. Some want this decision urgently and some do not. It is often very tempting to give advice to clients who seem to have such difficulty making choices that seem easy to the coach. Many clients have agonized over the decision and sought advice from people who know and care about them a great deal more than a coach might. It is very likely that they have received many suggestions.

Remember that the reason clients are talking to you is that either they have ignored all advice even though it was given with love and affection, it did not fit their view, it was not convincing, or the solution was not quite what they were looking for. Some clients even make a detailed list of pros and cons of one job offer versus another. When the number of items on the list is exactly the same in both columns, they feel stuck and unable to think outside the box. Even their own logic cannot convince them that one choice is better than then other. Therefore, make sure you do not give in to your temptation to offer advice prematurely. As with all coaching, the best answers are those that clients come up with on their own. Such decisions are ones they can live with for a long time.

The Myth of a Perfect Choice

Should I choose this job or that job? I am offered two jobs, both equally attractive, one in a big city and one in a small town. I do not know which place is better to live in. Should I stay with this company or go to another company? Should I break up with Tom and go with Fred? Should I get married or just stay in a committed relationship? Each choice has so much to offer and yet many clients seem unable to make any decision. It may seem like an easy choice. Many people will offer absolutely free advice and suggestions without being asked. People are usually generous that way.

When we meet such clients and listen to them carefully, they often hold several myths that seem to get in the way of making a decision. One of the major obstacles is that people tend to view the consequences of a decision as a life-or-death matter and believe that once they make a decision on an issue, they will never have another chance to change it. A common fear we hear is that the decision will affect them for the rest of their lives. Another difficulty we have observed is that clients want to make a perfect decision.

For example, a young, ambitious, highly intelligent client wanted to make a decision about his personal relationship with a girlfriend he was living with. He said he wanted to break off the relationship because he wanted to leave for California, but his dilemma was how to leave her without her realizing that he had left her! He could not bear her predictable reactions if he were to tell her about his wishes in person: tears, the pain and hurt of being rejected, pleading, and finally her effort to persuade him to stay in the relationship.

> **QUESTION FROM THE FIELD**
>
> "What about clients who are in denial?"
>
> We believe denial is in the eye of the beholder. The word *denial* is used to describe clients who disagree with the professional. We have found that describing a client as "in denial" is not a very useful concept. It usually takes the shape of confrontation, where the coach points out the misguided view of the client. In other words, there are right and wrong views. It is always better when clients decide their viewpoint is no longer working and that they need to do something different.

It is often this wish to make a decision without hurting or causing even the slightest pain or inconvenience to anybody in their lives that immobilizes clients. All decisions we make have consequences.

It is difficult, if not impossible, to make a perfect decision. Because the future is unknown and unknowable, which many wise people would say is a good thing, it is understandable why clients feel frozen in ice that may never melt. Another frequently observed difficulty is that clients generally look for ways to avoid possible unforeseen difficulties or potential problems or regrets instead of thinking about what the solution might look like.

So what is a coach to do?

- *Sense of humor.* Humor is a necessary and useful tool in coaching generally. It is especially helpful when meeting clients who tend to be serious and intensely focused on making the right decision. With the young man who wanted to leave his girlfriend without hurting her, the coach burst out laughing and asked, "Really? How are you going to do that?" The client also saw the absurdity of his thinking and broke out in loud laughter. Then he was able to collect his thoughts and said that his idea was not so good after all.
- *Big dose of curiosity.* The coach can lean forward, with eyes wide open, and say, "Really? Are you looking for a perfect solution? Wow!"

- *Use of suppose.* Handy little *suppose* can be helpful to learn clients' ideas of what will be different in their lives after they make a perfect decision. This works as a mini miracle question. Have clients describe the perfect outcome on both sides of the decision and have them scale how likely each outcome is. Of course, most clients end up laughing at their own absurdity.

> **QUESTION FROM THE FIELD**
>
> "The miracle question does not work well in decision situations. Clients say they still do not know which option to choose after the miracle."
>
> There are several ways to go about it. One possibility is to explore the miracle with several options, such as choosing one thing, choosing the other, a combination of both, or something completely different. Another usually helpful option is to explore the positive consequences of the decision, regardless of the choice.

- *Eyes on potential solutions, not risks.* Many clients are focused on what might get in the way; thus, their decision is often guided by what might create further problems. Unproductive effort is often directed at minimizing risks, not at opening up opportunities.
- *Use of scaling questions.* Ask the client to describe the solutions, opportunity, or possibilities opening up, rather than narrowing down of options. Scaling questions are very useful.

A Conversation About a Dilemma

Amy is a vivacious and attractive young woman, full of zest for life. At the time I met her, she already had a good job in the human resources department of a medium-sized corporation located in a medium-sized city. While attending a national conference recently, she met an executive of a larger company located in a larger and more attractive city who was looking for a director of human resources. It seemed natural that she would want to move to the bigger city, get a bigger salary, and move up to a director's position. This seemed like a dream come true.

But she had a dilemma. She had built a social network of good friends, close family, and a boyfriend who was not in a position to relocate to a new city because living there was more expensive. For weeks, Amy had been wracking her brain to figure out which way to go. Finally she decided that she was spinning her wheels, and the deadline to give a response was coming closer. Listen to the following dialogue to learn how a coach can help Amy make a good decision that she can live with.

Coach: Wow, you are in a tough situation, and I don't envy your position right now. How will you know that you have made a right decision?

Amy: I wish I knew. That's why I am talking to you. I've been going over this again and again, and nothing new comes up. I get the same "I don't know what to do" answer.

Coach: Suppose you make the right decision. I don't know yet how that's going to happen, but just suppose you made a decision that you could live with, maybe with small regrets once in a while that you should have taken the other way, but everybody thinks about that. How could you tell that?

Amy: Oh, are you saying that I will think about the other choice sometimes?

Coach: Of course, everybody does. Well, most everybody anyway.

Amy: My friends tell me that, too. I have been thinking about ways to put everything together to make a perfect decision, but since I made this appointment with you, I have been thinking about that. Maybe I won't be able to get everything right now.

Coach: Amazing. I'm sure you are right about that, I mean, not getting everything right now. Knowing this and having this wisdom, how will you know that the decision you make will be the right one for you for this stage of your life right now?

Amy: I suppose I might change my mind 2 years from now. What if I regret the decision I make?

Coach: Sure, you might, but then you would have learned so many things about yourself and your abilities in 2 years, and then it may not matter because you would face different challenges.

Amy: That would be nice. Even though you put it that way, I am still not able to answer your question. It is tough to make a decision because it feels like I should be able to look down the road 2 years from now.

Coach: Of course, everybody wishes we could see what's down the road. So I am going to ask you a strange question. Suppose a miracle happens tonight while you are sleeping and you wake up tomorrow morning with a very clear idea of what you want to do during the next 2 years. What would be different for you that will let you know that there was a miracle during the night?

Amy: I will wake up feeling refreshed, as if I had a good night's sleep. I will feel lighter in my body, maybe feel like dancing as I walk to the bathroom, and be able to look in the mirror and see myself clearly.

Coach: That's good. After you look at yourself in the mirror, what would you say to yourself?

Amy: Oh, I would say, Amy, you are a big girl now. It's time for you to take a risk and do something bold, like moving to another city and trying a job you never had before, be a director of human resources of a huge company. Find out what you can do and what you cannot do. You can always come back after 2 years.

Coach: That is taking a big risk. It's like a teenager leaving home and moving out on her own. So how could your boyfriend tell that there was a miracle for you?

Amy: Well, if I decide to take a risk, I guess he will have to take a risk too. If not, I will still go and learn something new about myself that I don't know now.

The conversation with Amy was a natural way to normalize her anxiety about the unknown. It was clear that she had been talking and listening to her friends, who gave her many suggestions and ideas. Therefore, it is always a good idea not to offer suggestions or ideas unless clients make a point of asking.

We are firm believers that life changes constantly and never stands still. Therefore, rather than enhancing fear of the unknown, following Amy's idea of a two-year commitment is an easily manageable way to make a bold decision. Direct and indirect compliments can be woven into the conversation, thus supporting and encouraging clients to be in control of their lives. We believe this is true empowerment.

CHAPTER FIVE

INFREQUENT BUT SERIOUS SITUATIONS

All coaching practitioners are, sooner or later, likely to run into situations that are not described in textbooks in neat, orderly, and tidy categories. Sometimes it is not easy to draw a clear line between goals and issues that are part of a perfectly normal life full of ups and downs. Life can be much messier than we would like it to be. Dealing with human life is very complex and at times it is too difficult to draw lines or package it into categories.

Not many coaching clients present a long list of problems, because they are, by and large, quite highly functioning and competent people who mostly want to improve and maximize their capacity to work smarter and not necessarily harder. Therefore, we decided to add a short chapter on infrequent situations that call for special care and sensitivity. We list here a new special situations that call for creativity and a great deal of supportive work.

Not all clients begin coaching with full disclosure of their problems and other challenging life issues, not because they are secretive and evasive but because many clients believe that certain aspects of their lives are not related to the coaching issues. They may need confidence to want to deal with issues and goals that they may not even have been aware of until the initial pressing issues are solved. Then they have more energy and ability to think about other issues or problems that have been nagging at them for a long time. Some clients find that as their work lives improve, other nagging problems may disappear and no longer be a concern. This is the beauty of brief coaching. A few other clients face crises that were totally unexpected. Both good and bad things happen to people.

Crises and unplanned emergencies happen to normal, healthy, and well-functioning people as well. Therefore, we believe that all coaches should know first aid measures for the most commonly faced problems that can show up in their practices. In this chapter, we address many of these difficult and special situations that will challenge your skills, and provide you with ways to manage them that, first of all, do no harm, and second, provide first aid that secures the appropriate help for the client. The ethical demands of coaching call for us to do what will be most helpful to clients first.

Occasionally we come across clients whose life experience is so horrific that they view life as a difficult struggle. They may have suffered intolerable and massive difficulties that not many people would have survived. Whether the client is in fact truly hopeless or is just hopelessly pessimistic is not the important point. What matters is that your client believes that he or she faces a hopeless situation and there appears to be no remedy. Therefore, as with any other client, you always need to work with the client's perceptions of reality and immediately address the issue of how he or she might have managed to survive the ordeal, when most people in similar situations might not have done as well. In such cases, coping questions can be very helpful. They are a useful tool that encourages clients to be optimistic and hopeful in

> **TOOLBOX**
>
> Coping questions include:
> I bet this is not easy.
> How do you manage to cope with the situation?
> What gives you even a little bit of hope for a light at the end of the tunnel?
> What has helped you keep going like this?

spite of their current difficult situations. A more detailed description of coping questions appears in Chapter 3 with strategies for coaching when clients report that things are worse.

WHEN A SETBACK OCCURS

It is common to have setbacks in life, either due to unanticipated events that are outside the client's control, or when clients face an entirely new situation. When this occurs, many clients and coaches tend to arrive at a conclusion that either they have failed or the coaching did not work. Neither is true, in most situations. Rather than viewing any setback as a failure or someone's shortcoming, a coach can calmly reassure the client that setbacks are a normal part of the changes they are making, as well as a normal part of life. Even though it may be two steps forward, and one step back, the client is still one step ahead of the game because in spite of the unforeseen events, at least things are not worse than when the client started. The setback can even indicate that one has not fallen down but is still standing up and even moving forward, although it may not be as fast as one would like. Nevertheless, it is still a move forward.

The following paragraphs detail steps to take if setbacks occur.

Stay calm. It is important for the coach to remain calm and not show shock or surprise. Ask the client to describe the setback. Ask about the details of what, who, where, when, and how to learn about the client's view of the setback as much as you can. Listen for any small successes in this description. For example, the client may usually yell and scream when he is upset about how his customer failed to come through with a large order, but somehow this time he managed to respond to disappointment in an unusual manner. He just walked out of the building for 5 minutes, took a deep breath, stretched, and then returned to his desk. You may want to find out how this occurred and what helped him so that he did not react in his usual way. Emphasize the small difference that he generated and ask the client to explain.

A young woman named Arlene loved her job working in the office of a trucking company but hated how her boss ranted and raved when his customers did not pay bills on time or any events outside the office affected his business negatively. Arlene was frightened whenever her boss went into one of these temper tantrums. Her goal for coaching was not only to keep her job, but also not to be intimidated by her boss so that she would not feel like she was walking on thin ice all day, long after the boss calmed down.

Arlene began her third session by saying that she was embarrassed to report that she had a big setback. She reported that, as usual, she could see another one of her boss's expressions of anger coming on. Having talked to the coach the week before, she was determined to respond to her boss calmly and be sympathetic, but she reported that she had failed to follow through on her plan. When the coach asked Arlene to describe her setback in detail, she said that even though she was determined not to let her boss's temper tantrum affect her, she found herself having old fears that reminded her of her father's temper and became so scared that she could hardly breathe. She first grew angry at herself, then at her boss for creating such turmoil in the office, and she finally walked out without saying anything. When she returned to work the next morning, she acted as if nothing had happened. She did not apologize for walking out on her boss or even mention the previous day's episode, primarily because she felt she had failed to stay calm and be sympathetic to her boss. To Arlene's surprise, however, her boss later apologized to her.

The coach highlighted Arlene's courage in walking out of the office, since in the past she had described herself as being frozen in fear. As the conversation continued, Arlene's confidence that she would be able to handle being mistreated in the future increased to 8.5. She decided that she did not need further coaching sessions for the time being, but that she might return later.

Ask about what helped to cope. Sometimes, indeed, some unfortunate events do happen in a client's life: losing a job, getting sick, having a care accident, attending a funeral, having a disaster that no one could have predicted or expected, and so on. Many events that could change our lives do happen without warning. Therefore, it is helpful to ask about what the client did to cope with unfortunate events. Again, listen for any kind of suggestion of new or different coping strategies. For example, on hearing what Arlene had done during her boss's most recent outburst, the coach had the following conversation with Arlene.

> **HOT TIP**
> No problem happens all the time.
> What happens the rest of the time?

Coach: Would you say this was different for you, walking out on your boss like you did?

Arlene: Yeah. Big difference. I have never done that before.

Coach: So where did you get the idea to walk away from the office, without saying anything? You are saying this is a big change for you.

Arlene: After I talked to you last time we met, I thought to myself, "Wait a minute, I don't need to put up with this. It is not my fault that he is having a temper tantrum and I don't need this." I thought the best thing is for me to just walk out and go home, and let him deal with his frustration with his customers.

Coach: Amazing. I am trying to picture the scenario. Saying to yourself "it is not my fault," and being able to walk away from this terrible scene. You are saying this is a big difference for you.

Arlene: Big time. I always took responsibility for people around me getting upset and thought that it was my job to calm them down and comfort them, but I was determined not to do that anymore.

Coach: Wonderful! How confident are you that you can do this again? What if your boss has another outburst? How confident are you that you will walk away again?

Arlene: I never heard him apologize to anyone before. I think other people at the office were as surprised as I was. I guess I can do it again since I've done it for the first time. Sure, on your scale, I would say about an 8.

Listen carefully for how resourceful and creative the client may have been in coping with such a difficult situation. Arlene not only coped with the difficulty but went one step further and made a big change for herself. That is, she felt that she did not have to comfort the upset person as well as trying to cope with her feeling that she might be somehow responsible. This is the resourcefulness and creativity that clients need to recognize so that their confidence in managing unpredictable events is increased. Even though she believed she had a setback in her ability to cope with her boss's unpredictable outbursts, the coach helped Arlene realize that she has moved beyond just coping and even created a big difference for herself.

Ask what the client needs to do to get back on track. Rather than limiting your work to admiring clients for their abilities to cope with difficult situations, you can lead the conversation to what the client needs to do to get back on track. It implies that the setback is just a slight detour in a client's life, and the client's attention needs to be refocused on the original goal of the coaching. Using scaling questions, ask about how confident clients are that they will be able to get back on track of staying focused on the original goal.

WHEN THERE IS NO PROGRESS

During training, case consultations, and supervision, we are often asked about an impasse in coaching, when the client reports no progress toward achieving goals. In addition, a coach may feel frustration at the lack of progress and it may feel like both the coach and the client are spinning their wheels or just standing still. If this is what you are experiencing, there are a couple of checkups you should do before blindly doing something just for the sake of doing something.

Focus on the Goal

Make sure to review whether the client's original goals are still valid. Since life moves at a rather rapid pace these days, it is easy to forget the initial goals that the client and the coach agreed on. Review your session notes and make sure you are focused on what the client said was important to him or her. If your review shows that you have strayed from the original goals, be honest with the client and make sure to check whether the initial goals are still relevant.

Use Scaling Questions

It is a good idea to reassess progress and renegotiate the goal, if needed:

Coach: I have been thinking that at this phase of coaching, I should do a mini checkup with you to make sure that we are on track. We have met four times since March, when we started. So I am going to ask you this way: when you first came to see me in March, remember you were quite upset? Remember how bad the situation was for you? That state of mind is at 1, and 10 would mean that your life is going reasonably well and that you are as confident as anybody could be to go on your own without further coaching. What number would you say your life generally is between 1 and 10 today?

Client: I would say, umm . . . between 7 and 8 . . .

Coach: Does that make it around 7.5?

Client: Yeah, I would say around that.

Coach: Great! What is different with your problem now that you are at 7.5?

Client: I have more confidence in myself that I can handle the situation with my procrastination. I just toss a coin and do what the coin tells me to do it has worked out fine so far.

This brief exchange shows how the coach helps the client evaluate and compare before and after pictures of himself and his lifelong tendency to procrastinate. The next step for the coach is to discuss ways to end the contact with the client (see Chapter 3).

Review

Because the client is the expert in assessing what is better or not, ask clients' help in reviewing what and how things are better for them. Listen carefully when the client describes the coaching experience. Again, scaling questions make the evaluation much more concrete and measurable, even intangible things like fears, hope, and life pressures. Because coaching is a subjective as well as objec-

> **TIP FROM THE FIELD**
> Explore with the client what or who could be a support to get back on track when there are setbacks.

206

tive experience for the client, it depends a great deal on his or her perception, rather than factual information.

Your review should include the goals of coaching. Was the goal realistic? Was the goal described in concrete, behavioral terms? Unless goal achievement is measurable or countable, it is difficult to know whether the goal has been achieved or not. Therefore, make sure that the goals are described in measurable terms. This will help guide the client to see whether coaching is working or not. Even if you began the coaching without a clear goal, do not worry. You can always get started by using scaling questions. Set the ending of coaching at 10 and 1 at the state of the problem when coaching began. Find out what the current number is and ask what needs to be done to move the number closer to 10. Be sure signs of 10 are described in concrete terms, as presence of solutions rather than an absence of problems. One can never go wrong by reviewing a successful period, even a short one, because remembering past success gives hope to clients that they can be successful again.

Look for Small Changes

It is unlikely that nothing has changed through coaching because we are always on the move and life never stands still but changes all the time. Therefore, in the unlikely event that the client perceives that nothing has changed, it is very likely that the client was looking for a large, drastic change just by coming to coaching. Therefore, it is time to look for small changes. Perhaps you have not made it clear to the client that changes come in small increments, not large packages. If the client was looking for large and drastic changes, of course he or she would be disappointed and it would seem like nothing much has changed.

When the Client Is Not Ready to Change

Because we are in a helping field, we can easily become more eager than clients to have their lives change for the better. At times, we can see that with a little more change, the client's life could be so much better that out of goodwill we may want more changes than clients want for themselves. Some clients may be quite content to change a little. For them, a little change may bring huge relief and they may want to just enjoy that relief for now. In such situations, make sure you are following the client's agenda, not your own.

Accept the Client's View

We want to repeat: It is a buyer's market and the customer is always right. Therefore, gracefully accept clients' views and allow them the right to decide what is good for them. Make sure not to impose your values on the client. Instead of viewing them as resistant, just accept their need to rest and enjoy their gains. Wait for a signal that they are ready for the next small changes. Do it with encouragement and graceful acceptance.

When the lack of progress seems to continue, you may need to seriously consider ethical issues. The coaching relationship is a contract between a client who needs and requests professional help and the coach, who gives an implied and direct message that he or she has the necessary skills and abilities to help the client with the presenting concerns. Therefore, it is imperative that the coach always checks and rechecks with clients about whether there is progress toward what the client is paying for. Along with the contractual nature of the relationship, there is also an ethical obligation not to mislead the client into paying for something that he is not actually getting. If the coach feels he or she is unable to live up to the contractual agreement, then the coach has an obligation to inform the client, discuss termination of the professional relationship, and refer the client to someone who can be more helpful. We cannot stress this point strongly enough.

CRISES AND EMERGENCIES

Even though it is unlikely that someone in coaching will come to you with a serious crisis or emergency, or serious substance abuse issues or life-threatening situations such as violence, it takes only a single episode of those rare situations to shake a coach's confidence. Therefore, it is a good idea to have some information on what to do in such a situation. We want to briefly address ways to provide first aid and then find further help the client may need.

An emotional crisis or emergency is considerably different from a physical emergency, when the safety of the person and the rapid delivery of first aid are the paramount concerns. Medical emergencies may be more obvious to observers. Most people manifest physical symptoms, signs of distress such as difficulty breathing, rapid pulse, elevated body temperature, and so on.

Emotional crises manifest in diverse ways. They can easily be misunderstood, especially when cultural differences play a role. Because there are greater variations in the expression of emotional crises, cultural familiarity plays a greatly enhanced role in assessing danger. But all coaches can learn to spot trouble and be supportive at a time of crisis. We provide a brief, but not comprehensive, guide for first aid when faced with such crises.

> **TIP FROM THE FIELD**
> You have heard that beauty is in the eye of the beholder. We have come to understand that denial is in the theory of the coach.

Crisis means some event or experience was totally unexpected, and the affected person is unprepared to deal with the episode. People caught in such events may panic or may look and behave as if they do not know what to do. They often report feeling lost. There are no immediate, ready-made solutions. The coach must improvise to fit the situation and provide what the client needs. It is easy to panic and make things worse, because emotional responses of the coach can exaggerate the client's behavior and may make the crisis worse than it would be otherwise.

- Stay calm. It is important to engage the brain more than the emotions at first. It is also easy and tempting to impose our solutions on clients because they appear stunned and seem to be incapable of thinking for themselves. Of course it is natural to be stunned, and it takes a while for anyone's intellectual capacity to kick in.
- Even though it may seem that the client is falling apart or is incapable of making intelligent decisions, that is not always the case.
- Many observers are often so stunned that they forget to ask something as simple as, "How long has it been since you ate last?" "Would you like a cup of coffee or tea?" "When was the last time you had something to drink?" These questions are all helpful to orient the client toward reality. Most people forget that when it has been a while since someone last ate or had anything to drink, cognitive function slows down considerably. Therefore,

make sure that the client is hydrated and also has had something to eat no longer than 3 or 4 hours ago. A coach should not assess someone's intellectual capacity at this stage.

- Ask what clients need immediately, right now, just to get through today or tonight. When we are not affected by crisis, it is easy to think about long-term solutions. But when the world has just turned upside down, clients can only think of short-term and concrete steps at the most basic level of coping. Make sure you plan to follow up at a designated time or that someone is available to support the victim.

- Ask about what has been helpful to cope with the crisis, even for a short time. It could be as little as 30 minutes since the crisis occurred. Find out what or who has helped to cope with the situation during the last 30 minutes. Clients can come up with amazing solutions.

For example, early one morning the headquarters office of a national restaurant chain called to ask for an emergency appointment for one of the managers. The corporation had hired the coach already to work with larger corporate issues and management coaching, and they were comfortable with the coach. The information given to the coach by the caller was that there was a terrible fire in one of the restaurants the night before and the fire destroyed the building. The caller said that the head manager of this restaurant, Mr. Gonzales, was in a state of shock and appeared to be in a catatonic state. The caller asked if the coach could see Mr. Gonzales right away because the office did not want to waste time looking for a therapist. Mr. Gonzales needed help immediately.

The coach, who had just come into the office to do some extra paperwork, was unprepared to see anyone for hours. Responding to the crisis, the coach said, "Yes, send him over to the office right now." Mr. Gonzales walked into the office as if he was exhausted and had not slept for days, half-dazed. But the coach was quite encouraged as soon as she learned that he drove his own car and found the right place on his own. The coach and Mr. Gonzales sat down and he described what happened. He had been a manager of this restaurant for several years and he was working the night before when the fire broke out. The fire department was called immediately and put out the fire with considerable water damage to the restaurant. Mr. Gonzales was not the owner but a hired manager and he was in such shock that he could hardly remember what happened.

The coach recognized that Mr. Gonzales was apparently able to drive home at night and then drive to the coach's office in the morning.

Coach: What a terrible night you must have had. What or who was most helpful for you to get through the night?

Mr. Gonzales: Yes, it was the most terrible night I ever had in my life and I am still shaking. I have to think about it a little bit. . . . I was just so thankful that nobody was hurt among my employees. . . . There was the fire department, water, water was everywhere . . . then the police came and I had to talk to so many people while I was trying to comfort and reassure the employees there . . .

Coach: So you were quite occupied last night. When did it finally hit you that you survived the fire?

Mr. Gonzales: I was just going through the motions, you know. Not until I got home, absolutely exhausted and numb from all the things that had to be done.

Coach: What would you say you did that was most helpful for you to get through the night?

Mr. Gonzales: I remember thinking as I walked into the house that it feels like 10 years have passed since I left the house early in the morning and went to work. Somehow I had this strange idea that I have to get my life back and so you know what I did? I went into the living room and sat down in my usual chair and held up last night's newspaper and acted like I was reading the paper. I sat there for a long time, pretending that I was reading. But you know, I couldn't see anything. It is my nightly routine, you know, I have my chair and read the paper before going to bed. I felt like I just had to do that.

Coach: I am impressed by how much you went through in one evening, but even more amazed that you were able to make yourself go through the nightly routine. Makes perfect sense to me.

Mr. Gonzales: Something about being in my living room and sitting in that chair was so helpful. At least something in my life didn't change and I needed to hang on to that.

Coach: Absolutely. Makes sense to me. In the middle of all the chaos and confusion, I am really impressed that you came up with something that made sense to you and comforted you. What else was helpful?

Mr. Gonzales: My wife. She was just wonderful. She usually talks a lot, but I just didn't want her to talk to me last night. I just needed to be alone and let it soak in. I want to make sure again that nobody was hurt, my workers, you know.

Mr. Gonzales was able to begin to think about other people in his surroundings, such as his wife and his employees. He described "getting back on my feet" as his next step. But first of all, he had to get to the restaurant and check on the damage to the building. He needed to talk to the police, insurance companies, and so on.

Ask whether the client can get helpful people to be helpful again. Find out who, when, where, and what has been most helpful in coping thus far and get clients to repeat the things that are helpful.

> **INTERESTING FACT**
>
> A study looked at clients who only came to a single therapy session.[*] Of the therapists, most guessed it had to do with something lacking so that the session was not successful, while 78% of the clients reported that the one session had helped them enough and there was no need to come back.

[*] Talmon, M. (1980). *Single session therapy: Maximizing the effect of the first (and often only) therapeutic encounter.* San Francisco: Jossey-Bass.

WAYS TO REFER THE CLIENT TO OTHER SERVICES

If the situation or problem is beyond your ability to help, it is always a good idea to refer the client to a professional who is better prepared to offer the service the client needs. Clearly, there are ethical and appropriate ways to suggest that your client follow up on the referral. Client follow-up is not always guaranteed, but the more careful discussion a coach has with the client about the referral, the more likely that the client will follow up on it and take advantage of different services.

Discuss the limits of your service. Openly and honestly explain that your training and experience are limited to coaching and the client's problem calls for skills beyond your training and ability to be helpful, and you believe that the client can be better served by someone with more experience with such problems. For example, the client may need a medical checkup or have health-related issues such as smoking cessation, drug- and alcohol-related problems, psychiatric issues and concerns, problems involving physical abuse, or serious marital and family issues. All of these problems require specialized training to be able to serve clients.

Make sure to ask clients how they feel about a referral and ask whether they have a preference for a male or female professional. Generally, giving clients a choice of whom to see is important. Discuss what each professional might bring to the client that you may not be able to provide. It is good idea to offer names and phone numbers of at least three people to refer the client to. Informed choice gives the best chance of a successful referral.

Ask what the client might want to get from the next professional. Also, ask what the client plans to do or think about to get the most out of the next contact. This helps clients prepare themselves to be active participants in the next course of intervention. Spending 5 or 10 minutes discussing the referral prepares clients to think about how they can play an active role in getting the right kind of help for themselves.

If the client has had previous experience with services for crisis intervention such as alcohol or drug problem treatment before, you may want to discuss what he or she needs to do differently so that this time the treatment experience is more positive.

HOW TO MAKE THE MOST OF A SINGLE SESSION

As we discussed in Chapter 2 in the story of the journalist in crisis, the initial presenting problem is a poor indicator of how many sessions a case might need. The modal number, the most frequent number of times a client comes to psychotherapy sessions, is one. Depending on the nature of the client population and the kind of problems one specializes in, somewhere between 30% and 40% of all new cases come to psychotherapy sessions one time only. Therefore, it is imperative that coaches know how to practice brief coaching. They must be able to work as if each session might be the last one. This is especially true with coaching clients, because almost all clients are employees or are self-employed, and the pressure to maintain a balance between work and personal life is a constant struggle. It should not come as a surprise to the coach if the client terminates coaching.

> **QUESTION FROM THE FIELD**
>
> "What do you say to a client who just lost his job and says his miracle would be to have the very same job back?"
>
> This is a very unhappy situation, and we wish we could make a miracle like that come true. We have had clients who have said this. We have also worked with spouses and parents who have wanted a medical miracle for their loved ones. In these situations, we think it is best to acknowledge the desire for this miracle. We cannot stop at that, however; we must move forward by asking, "On this miracle day, when you noticed you have your job back, what would you be doing?" "How would that help?" "Could doing something like that help now?"

Although intuitive sense might tell us that we should pack as much material as possible into a single session, coaches do the opposite. Working like a diamond cutter with precision technique, when a coach zeroes in on the key component that might create the greatest ripple effect, the result can be powerful.

So how does one know what might create

the greatest ripple effect in a client's life? Of course, we do not know it will work every time, but emphasizing the outcome that clients are seeking focuses their attention on what might be the key ingredient. Get in the habit of asking questions such as these:

- What is your best hope for this session?
- What needs to come out of this meeting today so that you would be able to say that it was a good thing to come and talk to me?
- What might your best friend say about how he or she could tell that this meeting with me today has been useful to you?

You may need to give clients a period of quiet time to collect their thoughts, because the outcome of coaching is usually not what most clients are prepared to discuss at the beginning.

CONCLUSIONS

Writing this book, as with all other books in the past, is all about examining our work, our thoughts, successes and failures of our practices. Writing forces us to reflect, think more clearly, and say and do what we do without much thinking in our daily life. That's the pain and joy of writing. It always leaves us with many small and big regrets, a cringe of embarrassment, feeling guilty that we have not been emotionally available to those who love us. Appreciation for families and friends who generously gave us time to devote to our work, yet feeling ourselves deprived of our time with them as well. And sharing our experience, some useful ideas, and lessons learned, with colleagues and with the field is what drives us to go through this writing process.

Every time we ask each other why are we doing this? Our thoughts invariably turn to what giving up time for writing is all about. Why are we doing this, with so much sacrifice, feelings of deprivation, pressures of meeting deadlines, and commitments to each other? Well, we must say it is all about our compassion for client's difficulties and dedication and desire to make a difference in someone's life: client's. Then our thoughts turn to all the lessons our clients have taught us.

As in any profession, our clients are the best teachers and trainers, and we need a mind-set that keeps us constantly learning from clients. This is the key to becoming better and better in our chosen field. Coaching is more an art than a science. The art of coaching is made up of being sensitive to other people's perspectives, becoming aware of their important social relationships, and learning ways to manage their relationships in the best ways possible. We want our clients to make good choices, not only so that they become more productive but also to promote their sense of well-being in their chosen way of living a good life. Skills can be learned and developed, but we believe the most important ingredient is the passion for improvement of our skills and compassion for others. We would like to add two more important characteristics.

Humility

As a wise person said, the more we learn, the more we become aware of how much more we need to learn. The longer we are in the field, the more we come to appreciate how much more there is to learn. This sense of willingness to learn comes from the humility to say to ourselves that we still have a great deal to learn. Of course, our best teachers are the clients with their pain and frustration, and our colleagues who share our sense of mission.

Curiosity

Rather than believing that we know everything already, a sense of innocent surprise and curiosity is what keeps us from becoming stagnant and stale. Infinite respect for our clients and curiosity about the many colorful and uniquely creative ways in which they find their own solutions is the most fascinating and at the same time satisfying aspect of working with people, rather than with things. We hope you also share our enthusiasm, passion, curiosity, and starry-eyed amazement at what people are capable of doing.

COACHING EXERCISES AND REMINDERS

SOLUTION BUILDING WITH MANDATED CLIENTS

I. Self-check: Set aside your personal biases about the client, if any. Set aside whatever you may have heard or read about the client from others. Be open to hearing the client's point of view. Find a way to maintain a "not-knowing" posture and curiosity.

II. Engage with the person first, not the problem.
    A. Connect with the person.
        • Find out what is important to the client.
        • Find out who is important to the client.
        • Learn the person's aspirations and dreams.
    B. Find out how to face the problem together with the client.
        • Put yourself one step behind the client (or side by side).

- Find out what the client is able and willing to do toward what he wants (exception-finding questions).

III. Negotiate for sustainable solutions.

    A. Find out details of what the client wants (not what the client does not want).

    B. Discuss past and recent successes in different social context (exceptions).

    C. What does the client need to do to repeat the exceptions? Ask "How did you do it?" or "How did you know it would work?"

    D. Remember useful questions: open-ended, miracle, exception-finding, scaling questions.

IV. Help the client assess progress toward goals.

    A. Ask many variations of scaling questions.

    B. Ask what is the next small step to achieve a desired small change.

    C. Find out how significant others would rate the client's progress.

    D. Ask what it would take to get closer to 10.

    E. Ask relationship questions often. (What would your friend say about where you are on the scale?)

    F. Use scaling questions, relationship questions; look for indications of exceptions.

CLIENT ENGAGEMENT

- Ask permission to do what we are going to do anyway. (How we do what we do makes a big difference.)
- Take what clients want (their goals) very seriously
- Spell out the coach's goals(agency, program) in simple, clear, and easy-to-understand language (get rid of jargon).
- If the above two seem contradictory, negotiate a resolution.
- Engage clients in achieving specific goals that are important to them.
- Use the client's key words throughout the conversation.
- Good engagement results in clients thinking differently.
- Keep in mind what and who are important to the client.
- Engagement is fragile and does not guarantee client compliance, but it is a necessary ingredient for a successful outcome.
- Inform the client about every step of what is happening and what may happen.

EARS: ELICIT, AMPLIFY, REINFORCE, START AGAIN

Elicit—Ask About Positive Changes

- What's been better, even a little bit? What have you been doing to make your life better? What has been your best day? How did that happen? Tell me about a time that you somehow avoided getting into trouble? What would your best friend say has been better for you?

Amplify—Ask for Details About Positive Change

- When did this happen? Tell me what happened? When? What else did you do? Who noticed it? How could you tell that they noticed? How did they respond? What did you do then? How did you know that was the right thing to do? How did that help? What do you know about yourself that tells you that you can do this again?

Reinforce—Make Sure the Client Notices and Values Positive Changes

- Nonverbal message: Lean forward, raise your eyebrows, or pick up a pen and take notes.

- Verbal message: Interrupt the client by asking, "Say that again?" or "You did what?" with an amazed look on your face.
- Compliments: Compliment the client for what has been accomplished. Even compliment the client for what has not been done by saying, "I'm glad you knew enough to go slowly," when the client did not do anything. Always find a way to uncover positive motives.

Start Again—Go Back to the Beginning and Focus on Client-Generated Changes

- What else has been better? How did you do that? How did that help? What difference did that make? What would your best friend (mother, boss, daughter, teacher, probabion officer, etc.) say about what you did?

COMPLIMENT AS INTERVENTION

Purpose

To help clients to notice what they do that is good for themselves as they move forward to achieve their goals in coaching.

Direct Compliment

A statement with a positive attribute.

Example: That's good! Amazing! I am glad you made it happen. I guess you
discovered that you knew all along that you could control yourself
even when you are so angry.

Type 1

When asking questions, notice the client's key words and
incorporate them into your next questions.

Example: How have you "managed" to make the "household so calm"?
What other times have you used your "small mouth"?

Note: this is a good way to develop a detailed picture
of the solution, with the client as your leading actor.

Type 2

Imply compliments through important relationships.

Example: What do you suppose the boss noticed that tells her that you are
making progress by coming here?
What would your boss say is the reason he keeps you in spite of the problems he had with you?
What would you notice that is different with your boss that tells you that
he really appreciates your hidden talent?

Type 3

Imply that clients know they are doing what is good for them.

Examples: Instead of saying, "That's good for you?," ask, "How did you decide that was good for you?" "How did you know that would help with your work?" "How did you figure out that it will work?" "What else do you know about yourself that tells you can make it this time?"

Common Rule

It is always a powerful and persuasive intervention to help clients discover their own resources and abilities.

A HEAD START IN BUILDING COOPERATION WITH CLIENTS: SOLUTION-BUILDING TOOLS

What

- Tell me what small accomplishments you are most proud of.
- What does that tell you about yourself?
- What is working best in your life right now?
- What would your best friend say about how you have made it happen?
- What would your best friend say is your three best qualities?
- What is your plan to use these best qualities?

- What will change about you then?
- What do you have to do to keep this change?
- What is the first small step you can take to make your life better?
- What will you do if you get the urge to fall back?
- What small step are you willing to take first? What else?
- What will you do then that you are not doing right now?
- What tells you that you are at 6?

Who

- Who have you learned most from about life? How did this person teach you? What else?
- Who do you count on for support? Who helps you out of trouble?
- Who will be the first to notice that you are different (making changes)?
- Who wants you here today? What do they want you to change?

When

- When do you show your best friend how proud you are about your successes (accomplishments)?

- When you begin to make the changes you want, what will be different?
- When will be a good time for you to take the first step?
- When you make these changes, who will be the first to notice?
- What would your best friend say will be different about you then?

Where

- Where did you decide you want to change your life?
- Where on the scale will you be when you finally make it back to school?
- Where will you be when you first notice a difference?
- Where on the scale do you want to be a year from now?

How

- How have you managed to survive so far?
- How do you decide to listen to your (valued person, best friend)?
- How do you know you can quit doing the thing that causes trouble?

- How have you made changes that you made in your life?
- How will you know that you are on track?
- How will you know this time it is the real thing? (go back to school, get back together after a breakup, etc.)
- How will you know what is the right thing to do?
- How badly do you want to make the necessary changes?
- How willing are you to work hard to get what you want in life?

Other Useful Beginnings

- Is there anything else that I forgot to ask that might be important to know?
- Is there anything else that you think I should know about you?
- Anything else? What else?
- You must have had a good reason to do what you did.

LEAD-IN POSSIBILITIES IN SOLUTION-BUILDING PRACTICE

Always make use of w-questions (what, when, where, who) but not *why* because of the negative or hostile tone it can convey. Use "How come?" instead. Your inflection should indicate curiosity, not a desire to educate the client.

How do you want your life to be different?	How can I be helpful?
How will things be different for you?	I wonder if you noticed?
What small change would you make?	How would that help?
I wonder what that would make?	Tell me more about . . .
What tells you that you can do this?	What would it take to . . . ?
I am not sure. What do you suppose . . . ?	Is it possible that . . . ?
What would your best friend say?	Did you notice . . . ?
How will you know things are getting better?	Suppose . . . just suppose . . .
How did you figure out how to do that?	How do you know?
Perhaps . . .	Anything else?
What difference would it make?	It seems like . . .
Did I hear you right?	It is amazing!

When things are different, what would you do then that you are not doing right now?	
What else would change?	I don't know . . . yet.
What is better?	What else is better?
What do you have to do to keep your 6?	How confident would your best friend be that you will stay at 6 this time?

USEFUL LANGUAGE SKILLS

- *Not-knowing* skills—Maintain a posture of curiosity and ability to set aside our expertise and listen.
- *Client's key words*—Use key words to formulate next question.
- *Suppose*—"Suppose your frustration is resolved, what . . ."
- *Different, difference*—"What difference would it make? Is (was) it different for you? Who would notice the difference?"
- *Good reasons*—"You must have a good reason to be . . ."
- "What would you (he, she, they) do instead?"
- *Relationship questions*—"What would your best friend say . . ."

- "How helpful is that? How would that be helpful?"
- *Tentative language* (collaborative stance).
- Responsibility for change versus blame for mistakes.

INDEX

Brief Coaching: Taken More Seriously
A DVD for coaches
by Peter Szabó and Insoo Kim Berg

In this DVD, viewers will be introduced to Jonathan, the founder and director of a company which has been in business for ten years. Overwhelmed by daily business issues Jonathan wants to be "taken more seriously" by board members and colleagues at his company as he pursues some of his long-standing dreams. Szabó demonstrates how to coach clients like Jonathan and guide them in their efforts to get back on track and moving toward their goals. In the session presented in the DVD, Szabó and Berg show the effectiveness of providing Jonathan with "a concentrated time to think" about his goals, resources, and next steps. Berg concludes with an immediate post-session interview that allows viewers to learn what has been most helpful to Jonathan. There is also footage of a later session with Jonathan in which he discusses the further progress he has made in pursuing his dreams.

Brief Coaching: Taken More Seriously features:

Part 1) Coaching Session (34.09)
Part 2) Thinking Break (5.52)
Part 3) Feedback to Client (2.32)
Part 4) Post Session Interview (7.55)
Part 5) Follow-up Session (3.53)
Total running time 53 minutes

$100 USD (plus shipping) • MacIntosh and PC compatible • Total running time 53 minutes

Order by mail:

B F T C
P.O. Box 13736
Milwaukee, WI 53213-0736
USA

Order by phone or email:

Phone : 414-302-0650
e-mail : briefftc@aol.com

Make out your check to "BFTC"